KU-765-117

www.wit@wisdom

Summersdale Publishers Ltd
46 West Street
Chichester
West Sussex
PO19 1RP
United Kingdom

www.summersdale.com

Printed and bound in Great Britain by
Cox & Wyman Ltd, Reading, Berkshire

ISBN 1 84024 104 7

www.wit@wisdom

compiled by Gerd de Ley & David Potter

SUMMERSDALE

The twentieth century [was] only the nineteenth
speaking with a slightly American accent

Philip Guedalla

At the end of any length of time, a year, a decade or even a century, we tend to need to review that period chronologically and to highlight the main events. Language and communication is central to all our lives, so it seemed like a good idea to us to review the way that twentieth century authors, politicians, actors, philosophers and 'celebrities' have defined both new and older words and expressions.

Regular dictionaries, as grammatically accurate as they are, fail truly to represent the normal changes that occur in widely used and spoken language – colloquialisms, phrases and so-called compound words are glossed over. With a new century and millennium ahead of us, this review lays out, for posterity, our idiosyncrasies and expressions and reflects the changes in our cultures.

The definitions in this book will not help you to pass an exam or perfect your letter writing skills. Rather they are contemporary thoughts to muse and amuse, to raise a smile and with which to agree or disagree.

Accordingly, this collection contains serious definitions, *double entendres*, puns and even absurdities. There are definitions of words little used, standard and brand new – but all are defined with an interesting twist.

We hope that reading and using these definitions gives you half the pleasure it gave us to collect them. After all, isn't a quotation nothing more than 'a handy thing to have about, saving one from the trouble of thinking for oneself' (A A Milne)?

Gerd de Ley and David Potter

Definitions belong to the definer – not the defined
Toni Morrison
Beloved, 1987

Everything has to be defined. Yet how can you define anything except by its limitations?
David Storey
Arnold Middleton, 1959

To define is to exclude and negate
José Ortega y Gasset
The Modern Theme, 1923

ability – the art of getting credit for all the home runs someone else hits
Casey Stengel

abortion – a skilfully marketed product sold to a woman at a crisis in her life. If the product is defective, she can't return it for a refund
Carol Everett
– mechanical rape
Olivia Gans
– to correct a misconception
Dave Krieger

above – down when standing on your head
Harry Mulisch

abstract art – a product of the untalented, sold by the unprincipled to the utterly bewildered
Al Capp
(see also *art, modern art, work of art*)

absolute truth – the thing that makes people laugh
Carl Reiner

absurd – every opinion that differs from ours
Augusto Gil

abut – the highpoint for a leg man
H Gordon Havens

accent – something other people have
Colin Bowles

acceptance – the courage of the losers
Frans de Wilde

accident – a child conceived long after your husband's vasectomy
Cy DeBoer

accordion – a piano with suspenders
Piet Grijs

accountant – someone who can put two and two together to make a living
Colin Bowles
– a man hired to explain that you didn't make the money you did
Maxim Drabon
– *pl.* the witch-doctors of the modern world, willing to turn their hands to any kind of magic
Justice Herman

acme – delivery truck you don't want to see arriving on your twenty-fifth anniversary
Cy DeBoer

acquaintance – somebody you nod to if he nods first
Mignon McLaughlin

acrobat – a guy who goes around with a chap on his shoulder
Milton Berle

acting – a matter of giving away secrets
Ellen Barkin
– experience with something sweet behind it
Humphrey Bogart
– a matter of calculated instinct
Ernest Borgnine
– the expression of a neurotic impulse
Marlon Brando
– the shy person's revenge on the world
Sinead Cusack
– happy agony
Alec Guinness
– a way of living out one's insanity
Isabelle Huppert
– a demonstration of rebellion against the mundanity of everyday existence
Michèal MacLiammoir
– a question of absorbing other people's personalities and adding some of your own experience
Paul Newman
– a masochistic form of exhibition
Laurence Olivier
– farting about in disguise
Peter O'Toole
– not being emotional, but being able to express emotion
Kate Reid
– the ability to keep an audience from coughing
Ralph Richardson
– standing up naked and turning around very slowly
Rosalind Russell

– an attempt to find universality, reality and truth in a world of pretending
George C Scott
– shouting in the evening
Patrick Troughton
action – the antidote to despair
Joan Baez
– the only answer to conquer fear
Norman Vincent Peale

actor – a man who tries to be everything but himself
Milton Berle
– a high tree that catches a lot of wind, and then he bends
Herman de Coninck
– *pl.* a race apart, doomed to go through life pretending to be somebody else
R F Delderfield
– person with a regrettable number of psychological problems
Tony Dunham
– a guy who if you ain't talkin' about him, ain't listening
George Glass
– a kind of unfrocked priest who, for an hour or two, can call on heaven and hell to mesmerise a group of innocents
Alec Guinness
– a hero that feeds himself with applause
Karel Jonckheere
(see also *cinema, film, Hollywood, star, theatre*)

actor-manager – one to whom the part is greater than the whole
Ronald Jeans

actress – *pl.* another kettle of bitch
Gilbert Harding
– someone with no ability who sits around waiting to go on alimony
Jackie Stallone
– someone who wears boa feathers
Sigourney Weaver
(see also *cinema, film, Hollywood, starlet, theatre*)

actuary – someone who cannot stand the excitement of chartered accountancy
Glan Thomas

Adam – God's finger-exercise before he created Eve
Jeanne Moreau
– the first accomplice
Jacques Prévert

adjectives – the potbelly of poetry
R Z Sheppard

adjucation – a legal game in which courts try to find where legislatures have hidden justice
Edmund H Volkart
admiral – a general with sea legs
Delfeil de Ton

admiration – jealousy in an evening dress
Fernand Lambrecht

adolescence – the age when a girl's voice changes from no to yes
Joey Adams
– nature's way of preparing parents to welcome the empty nest
Patricia Adams & Karen Savage
– the stage of growth that turns a perfectly normal child into an alien
Joyce Armor
– that period when a young man would never believe that someday he will become bald
O A Battista
– the stage between pigtails and cocktails
Milton Berle
– the period between puberty and adultery
Jasmine Birtles
– the time when you are always starting things you can't finish – like phone calls
Bob O'Driscoll
– that period in a child's life when his parents become most difficult
Ryan O'Neal
– the age at which children stop asking questions because they know all the answers
Jan Opalach
– a time when people worry about things there's no need to worry about
Katherine Anne Porter
– a tiresome period of transition between childhood and adulthood, bearing the pain of both and the joy of neither
Edmund H Volkart
(see also *teenager*)

adolescents – children old enough to dress by themselves if they could just remember where they last saw their clothes
Peter Darbo

adornment – a reflection of the heart
Coco Chanel

adult – a child blown up by age
Simone de Beauvoir
– *pl.* obsolete children
Theodor Seuss
– caricature of a child
François Truffaut
– child without a future
Toon Verhoeven
adultery – what takes so little time and causes so much trouble
John Barrymore
– doing the right thing with the wrong person
Colin Bowles
– the application of democracy to love
H L Mencken

adult western – one in which the hero still loves his horse, only now he's worried about it
Henny Youngman

adventure – the vitaminizing element in histories both individual and social
William Bolitho

advertisements – the cave art of the twentieth century
Marshall McLuhan

advertiser – the overrewarded court jester and court pander at the Democratic court
Joseph Wood Krutch

advertising – the very essence of democracy
Bruce Barton
– what you do when you can't go to see somebody
Fairfax Cone
– the most fun you can have with your clothes on
Jerry Della Femina
– the science of arresting the human intelligence for long enough to get money from it
Stephen Leacock
– a valuable economic factor because it is the cheapest way of selling goods, especially if they are worthless
Sinclair Lewis
– the greatest art form of the twentieth century
Marshal McLuhan

advertising

– the place where the selfish interests of the manufacturer coincide with the interests of society
David Ogilvy
– the rattling of a stick inside a swill bucket
George Orwell
– capitalism's soft sell
Sue Sharpe
– the art of making whole lies out of half truths
Edgar A Shoaff
– selling in print
Daniel Starch
– the vision which reproaches man for the paucity of his desires
E S Turner
– legalised lying
H G Wells

advertising agency – eighty-five per cent confusion and fifteen per cent commission
Fred Allen

advice – what we ask for when we already know the answer but wish we didn't
Erica Jong
– always a confession
André Maurois
– an uncertain gift
Jeffrey Whitney

aerobic exercises – exercise to the brink of cardiac arrest
Russell Ash

aerobics – comes from two Greek words: aero, meaning 'ability to,' and bics, meaning 'withstand tremendous boredom'
Dave Barry
– gay folk dancing
Bruce Smirnoff

aesthete – a forlorn, arty person who professes to worship beauty, but never seems to find the right church
Edmund H Volkart

aesthetic value – often the by-product of the artist striving to do something else
Evelyn Waugh

Afrikaans – a language that sounds like Welsh with attitude and emphysema
A A Gill

after dinner speech – an occupation monopolised by men – women can't wait that long
Steve Miller

afternoon snack – the pause that refleshes
Mary B Michael

age – something that doesn't matter, unless you are a cheese
Billie Burke
– a question of mind over matter. If you don't mind, it doesn't matter
Dan Ingman
– a slowing down of everything except fear
Mignon McLaughlin
– the elasticity of a person's intelligence and the longevity of that elasticity
Rod Steiger
– a high price to pay for maturity
Tom Stoppard
(see also *middle age, old age*)

AIDS – this generation's Vietnam
Richard Goldstein
– code name for privacy
Freek de Jonge

airline travel – hours of boredom interrupted by moments of stark terror
Al Boliska

airplane – flying ship considered by most studies to be the safest mode of transportation, at least when it remains aloft
Rick Bayan

airport – a free-range womb
Brigid Brophy

alabaster – an illegitimate Arab
Milton Berle

alarm clock – an object used to wake up people who don't have children
Mel Allen

alas – early Victorian for *oh, hell*
Oliver Herford

alcohol – an extremely stable chemical – until you drink it
O A Battista
– the anaesthesia by which we endure the operation of life
George Bernard Shaw

alcoholic – a man who drinks more than his own doctor
Alvan L Barach
– someone you don't like who drinks as much as you do
Dylan Thomas

alcoholic psychosis – DTs in a dinner suit
Kin Hubbard

alcoholism – the intermediate stage between socialism and capitalism
Norman Brenner

Alderney – a great spinach omelette off the coast of France
Miles Kington

Muhammad Ali – the Jackie Onassis of the sweat set
John Leonard

alibi – a reason with a bad reputation
Doug Larson

alimony – the high cost of leaving
Joey Adams
– something like buying oats for a dead horse
Arthur Baer
– giving comfort to the enemy
Milton Berle
– bounty after the mutiny
Johnny Carson
– the root of all evil
Jilly Cooper
– billing minus cooing
Mary Dorsey
– a system whereby, if two people make a mistake, one of them continues to pay for it
Peggy Joyce
– the curse of the writing classes
Norman Mailer

– the ransom that the happy pay to the devil
H L Mencken
– the royalties that go with a divorce
Hugo Olaerts
– a life sentence for not committing a murder
Alexander Pola
– always having to say you're sorry
Philip J Simborg
– the screwing you get for the screwing you got
Chris Szurgot

allies – tomorrow's enemies
Edmund H Volkart

almost – a word that sticks in the throat like failure
David McCallum

aluminium – precious metal to men who drink beer by the six-pack
Cy DeBoer

alumni – a group of college graduates who attend football games on Saturday to find reasons to fire the coach on Monday
Jimmy Cannon

amateur – Sunday driver of the arts
Robert Lembke

ambition – the noble name one gives to his money problems
Philippe Bouvard
– the grand enemy of all peace
John Cowper Powys
– a poor excuse for not having sense enough to be lazy
Charlie McCarthy
– the immemorial weakness of the strong
Vita Sackville-West

amend – to rewrite a law in such a way as to further obscure its already confused meaning
Edmund H Volkart

America – the country where you buy a liftetime supply of aspirin for one dollar, and use it up within two weeks
John Barrymore
– the only country in the world where beauty is more celebrated than talent
O A Battista

america

– the land of permanent waves and impermanent wives
Brendan Behan
– a place where Jewish merchants sell Zen love beads to agnostics for Christmas
John Burton Brimer
– the best half-educated country in the world
Nicholas Murray Butler
– the only country left where we teach languages so that no pupil can speak them
John Erskine
– the greatest law factory the world has ever known
Charles Evans Hughes
– a mistake, a gigantic mistake
Sigmund Freud
– one of the finest countries anyone ever stole
Bobcat Goldthwait
– the only country deliberately founded on a good idea
John Gunther
– a society which believes that God is dead but Elvis is alive
Irv Kupcinet
– the glory, jest, and terror of mankind
James M Minifie
– a country that has leapt from barbarism to decadence without touching civilization
John O'Hara
– a country that doesn't know where it is going, but is determined to set a speed record getting there
Laurence J Peter
– the only country where a housewife hires a woman to do her cleaning so she can do volunteer work at the day nursery where the cleaning woman leaves her child
Bob Phillips
– a nation that conceives many odd inventions for getting somewhere but can think of nothing to do when it gets there
Will Rogers
– the only country in the world where people jog ten miles a day for exercise, then take elevators up to the mezzanine
Joel Rothman
– a country where law and customs alike are based on the dream of spinsters
Bertrand Russell
– the greatest of opportunities and the worst of influences
George Santayana
– an enormous frosted cupcake in the middle of millions of starving people
Gloria Steinem
– just a nation of two hundred million used-car salesmen with all

the money we need to buy guns and no qualms about killing anybody else in the world who tries to make us uncomfortable
Hunter S Thompson
– a large friendly dog in a small room. Every time it wags its tail it knocks over a chair
Arnold Toynbee
– the only country in the world where failing to promote yourself is regarded as being arrogant
Garry Trudeau
– a vast conspiracy to make you happy
John Updike
– somewhat like Palestine before Christ appeared – a country full of minor prophets
Peter Ustinov
– the country with the highest number of psychiatrists
Georges van Acker
– a land where a citizen will cross the ocean to fight for democracy – and won't cross the street in a national election
Bill Vaughan
– God's Crucible, the great Melting-Pot where all the races of Europe are melting and re-forming
Israel Zangwill
– a nation of laws: badly written and randomly enforced
Frank Zappa

American artist – the unwanted cockroach in the kitchen of a frontier society
John Sloan

American democracy – the inalienable right to sit on your own front porch, in your pyjamas, drinking a can of beer and shouting out 'Where else is this possible?'
Peter Ustinov

American food – a plenitude of peanut butter and a dearth of hot mustard
Patrick Dean

American football – committee meetings separated by outbreaks of violence
George F Will

American government – a rule of the people, by the people, for the boss
Austin O'Malley

American male – the world's fattest and softest; this might explain why he also loves guns – you can always get your revolver up
Gore Vidal

American presidency – a Tudor monarchy plus telephones
Anthony Burgess

Americans – they are and they have, but they don't behave
A de Froe
– the only people in the world whose status anxiety prompts them to advertise their college and university affiliations in the rear window of their automobiles
Paul Fussell
– people who laugh at African witch-doctors and spend 100 million dollars on fake reducing systems
L L Levinson
anarchism – a game at which the police can beat you
George Bernard Shaw

anarchy – the purpose of those who have nothing to lose
Ernst R Hauschka

anatomy – something everyone has, but which looks better on a girl
Bruce Raeburn

anchorperson – a bland, well-coiffed TV entertainer who is paid more to read the news than ten reporters are paid to report it
Rick Bayan

anecdote – a joke in evening dress
Paul Jacobs

Anglo-Irishman – a Protestant with a horse
Brendan Behan

anno domini – the most fatal complaint of all in the end
James Hilton

answer – a form of death
John Fowles
– the best way of killing a question
Wim Triesthof

Antarctica – Snowman's land
L L Levinson

anthologist – a lazy man who likes to spend a quiet evening at home reading good books
Dorothy Parker

antidotes – what you take to prevent dotes
Art Linkletter

anti-feminist – the man who is convinced that his mother was a fool
Rebecca West
(see also *feminist*)

antique – an object that has made a round trip to the attic
Joey Adams
– something that's been useless so long it's still in pretty good condition
Franklin P Jones
– yesterday's kitsch at today's prices
Jacques Tati

anti-semitism – a noxious weed that should be cut out. It has no place in America
William Howard Taft

anxiety – that condition in which, waiting for the unspeakable, we face the undo-able
Mignon McLaughlin

apartheid – a subtle form of genocide
Allan Aubrey Boesak

apathy – the glove into which evil slips its hand
Bodie Thoene

apéritif – a set of dentures
Spike Milligan
– the evening prayer of the French
Paul Morand

aphorism – the swallow of the art of reason
Eugenio d'Ors
– *pl.* key to experiences and vice versa
Sigmund Graff
– the 'amen' of an experience
Hans Kudszus
– a fart from the brains
Georges Perros

apology – a good way to have the last word
Peter Darbo
– the superglue of life: it can repair just about anything
Lynn Johnston

appeal – when you ask one court to show its contempt for another court
Finlay Peter Dunne

appeaser – *pl.* people who believe that if you keep throwing steaks to a tiger, the tiger will turn vegetarian
Heywood Broun
– one who feeds a crocodile hoping it will eat him last
Winston Churchill

appetite – luxury edition of hunger
Anita

applause – the custom of showing one's pleasure at beautiful music by immediately following it with an ugly noise
Percy A Scholes

appreciation – the memory of the heart
Bill Beattie

après ski – most men think it means Before-Bed
Monique Lacour

Arab – a Greek on a camel
Colin Bowles

archbishop – a Christian ecclesiastic of a rank superior to that attained by Christ
H L Mencken

archeology – science without a future
Georges Elgozy

architect – a specialist, designing space for man in accordance with nature
Henry Buszko & Aleksander Franta
– a servant, a tailor, who cuts and measures the thin chap or the fat chap and tries to make him comfortable
Basil U Spence

architecture – building plus delight
Ove Arup

– the art of creating a space
Yoshinobu Ashihara
– inhabited sculpture
Constantin Brancusi
– mainly a question of overcoming certain practical problems
Harald Deilmann
– the art which acts the most slowly, but the most surely, on the soul
Ernest Dimnet
– a machine for the production of meaning
Arata Isozaki
– the art of how to waste space
Philip Johnson
– the thoughtful housing of the human spirit in the physical world
William O Meyer
– the most inescapable of the higher arts
Anthony Quinton
– art you can walk through
Dan Rice
– a history book without lies
Robert Sabatier
– the will of an epoch translated into space
Ludwig Mies Van Der Rohe
(see also *postwar architecture*)

argument – the longest distance between two points of view
Dan Bennett
– the hereditary misfortune of thought
Elias Canetti

aristocracy – rectitude, platitude, high-hatitude
Margot Asquith

arms (*weaponry*) – adult toys
Jean Follain

army – a body of men assembled to rectify the mistakes of the diplomats
Josephus Daniles

aroma – a smell described by a bore
Henry Beard

arrival – the start of a departure
Robert Sabatier

arsonist – a man with a burning desire
Ethel Meglin

art – a fight against decay
Brian Aldiss
– the artist's false catholicism, the fake promise of an afterlife and just as fake as heaven and hell
Woody Allen
– an attempt to integrate evil
Simone de Beauvoir
– the apotheosis of solitude
Samuel Beckett
– a challenge to despair
E C Bentley
– a way of seeing
Thomas Berger
– the only thing that can go on mattering once it has stopped hurting
Elizabeth Bowen
– a lie that uncovers the truth
Jeroen Brouwers
– a self-respecting search for the unknown
Eugenio Carmi
– the unceasing effort to compete with the beauty of flowers – and never succeeding
Marc Chagall
– nature speeded up and God slowed down
Malcolm de Chazal
– the triumph over chaos
John Cheever
– a marriage of the conscious and the unconscious
Jean Cocteau
– the conscious apprehension of the unconscious ecstasy of all created things
Cyril Connolly
– the most frenzied orgy a man is capable of
Jean Dubuffet
– everything that men call art
Dino Formaggio
– significant deformity
Roger Fry
– a way of possessing destiny
Marvin Gaye
– a subject metamorphosed into an object
Nicholas Ghika
– a collaboration between God and the artist, and the less the artist does the better
André Gide

– the immeasurable translated into terms of the measurable
Eric Gill
– a creative connection to the past and the present
Sam Gilliam
– a force which blows the roof off the cave where we crouch imprisoned
Ernest Hello
– the objectification of feeling, and the subjectification of nature
Suzanne K Langer
– the only form of progress that uses equally well the paths of truth and lies
Jean Marie Le Clézio
– thoughtful workmanship
W R Lethaby
– an appeal to a reality which is not without us but in our minds
Desmond MacCarthy
– that what evokes the mystery without which the world would not exist
René Magritte
– that through which form becomes style
André Malraux
– the great refusal of the world as it is
Herbert Marcuse
– to give different answers to the same questions
Theo Mestrum
– the difference between seeing and just identifying
Jean Mary Norman
– the imposing of a pattern on experience, and our aesthetic enjoyment is recognition of the pattern
Alfred North Whitehead
– an assertive statement of an evolving self
Sondra O'Neale
– the demonstration that the ordinary is extraordinary
Amédée Ozenfant
– a form of catharsis
Dorothy Parker
– the lie that enables us to realize the truth
Pablo Picasso
– the undoing of the world of things
Max Raphael
– the reasoned derangement of the senses
Kenneth Rexroth
– a distillation – a moment amplified, magnified
Ken Russell
– everything the artist spits
Kurt Schwitters

– humanized science
Gino Severini
– the signature of civilization
Beverly Sills
– a border of flowers along the course of civilization
Lincoln Steffens
– a noble effort to illustrate truth
Guy Stevens
– the affirmation of life
Alfred Stieglitz
– the only way to run away without leaving home
Twyla Tharp
– the terms of an armistice signed with fate
Bernard de Voto
– communication spoken by man for humanity in a language raised above the everyday happening
Mary Wigman
– man's attempt to communicate an understanding of art to man
Christopher Wilmarth
– making something out of nothing and selling it
Frank Zappa
(see also *abstract art, modern art, work of art*)

art critics – failed artists, like most artists
Paul Citroen
(see also *critic, good critic, reviewmanship*)

arthritis – twinges in the hinges
G B Howard

artificial insemination – procreation without recreation
Rick Bayan

artificial intelligence – the art of making computers that behave like the ones in movies
Bill Bulko
(see also *intelligence*)

artist – a perceptual window
Jack Chambers
– a member of the leisured classes who cannot pay for his leisure
Cyril Connolly
– the seismograph of his age
Robert W Corrigan
– a creature driven by demons. He doesn't know why they chose him and he's usually too busy to wonder why
William Faulkner

– the medium between his fantasies and the rest of the world
Federico Fellini
– not a mirror to reflect the world, but a hammer with which to shape it
Vladimir Mayakovsky
– *pl.* the unacknowledged legislators of the world
Jonathan Miller
– a dreamer consenting to dream of the actual world
George Santayana
– somebody who produces things that people don't need to have but that he – for *some reason* – thinks it would be a good idea to give them
Andy Warhol
(see also *American artist, primitive artist*)

art of conversation – not only to say the right thing in the right place, but to leave unsaid the wrong thing at the tempting moment
Dorothy Nevill
(see also *conversation, good conversation*)

art of flying – to throw yourself at the ground and miss
Douglas Adams
(see also *flying*)

art of living – the art of knowing how to believe lies
Cesare Pavese
(see also *living*)

art of love – knowing how to combine the temperament of a vampire with the discretion of an anemone
E M Cioran
(see also *eternal love, fall in love, first love, ideal love, love, platonic love, true love*)

art of politics – directing rationally the irrationalities of men
Reinhold Niebuhr
(see also *politics*)

art of teaching – is only the art of awakening the natural curiosity of young minds for the purpose of satisfying it afterwards
Anatole France
(see also *good teaching, teaching*)

art of writing – the art of applying the seat of the pants to the seat of the chair
Mary Heaton Vorse

– the art of erasing
Julian Przybos
(see also *major writing, writing*)

art school – a place for young girls to pass the time between high school and marriage
Thomas Hart Benton

ass – the face of the soul of sex
Charles Bukowski

assassination – the extreme form of censorship
George Bernard Shaw

associate producer – the only guy in Hollywood who will associate with a producer
Fred Allen
(see also *cinema, film, Hollywood, producer*)

assumption – the mother of screw-up
Angelo Donghia
– *pl.* the termites of relationships
Henry Winkler

astrology – an ancient pseudoscience and bar-room conversation-starter founded on the premise that everyone born under the same star will meet a dark stranger, receive a propitious business offer or suffer an attack of dyspepsia on the same day
Rick Bayan

astronaut – a man who doesn't have to bring along something for his wife
Robert Lembke
– *pl.* Rotarians in outer space
Gore Vidal
(see also *budding astronaut*)

atheist – a man who has no invisible means of support
John Buchan
– someone who refuses to give God the benefit of the doubt
C Buddingh'
– a guy who watches a Notre Dame versus SMU football game and doesn't care who wins
Dwight D Eisenhower
– someone who believes he has no belief
Georges Elgozy

– one who hopes the Lord will do nothing to disturb his disbelief
Franklin P Jones
– one who does not believe in God but is still holier than thou
L A Rollins
– a man who believes himself an accident
Francis Thompson
(see also *dead atheist*)

atom bomb – an explosive device under which all people are cremated equal
Joel Rothman
– a paper tiger which the United States reactionaries use to scare people
Mao Tse-Tung
(see also *neutron bomb, tactical nuclear weapon*)

atomic war – herald of total peace
Ron Kritzfeld

attractive – just not beautiful enough
Theo Mestrum

audiences – just coughing bastards
Donald Wolfit

Australia – a land of harsh rules, which everyone breaks
Jilly Cooper
– a huge rest home, where no unwelcome news is ever wafted on to the pages of the worst newspapers in the world
Germaine Greer
– the only country in the world where the word 'academic' is regularly used as a term of abuse
Leonie Kramer

Australian – someone who is too drunk to feel his sunburn
Colin Bowles
– *pl.* living proof that aborigines screw kangaroos
John Freeman

Austria – Switzerland speaking pure German with history added
J E Morpurgo

author – the mother of a book
Johan Daisne
(see also *co-author, freelance writer, novelist, professional writer, screenwriter, writer*)

authority – a high hat under which every donkey can hide his ears
Antoon Vloemans

autobiography – *pl.* alibi-ographies
Clare Boothe Luce
– an obituary in serial form with the last instalment missing
Quentin Crisp
– the last refuge of scoundrels
Henry Gray
– a pre-emptive strike against biographers
Barbara Grizutti Harrison
– an unrivalled vehicle for telling the truth about other people
Philip Guedalla
– an absorbing work of fiction, with something of the charm of a cryptogram
H L Mencken
– a book of gossip about other people
J B Morton

auto insurance – the only kind of insurance for which the premiums get higher the younger you are
O A Battista
(see also *insurance, life insurance*)

automatic – means that you can't repair it yourself
Mary H Waldrip

autumn – a second spring when every leaf is a flower
Albert Camus
– a season followed immediately by looking forward to spring
Doug Larson
– a damp spring
Katina Papa
– when leaves slowly turn from green to brown to gold to litter
Joel Rothman

avant-garde – the one thing constant in a changing world
Louis Jouvet
– French for off-Broadway garbage
Dick van Dyke

average – general appraisal of other people's kids
Cy DeBoer

average man – one who waits for the first snow before putting antifreeze in his radiator
O A Battista

– a guy who spends his whole life trying to prove to everybody that he isn't
Harvey Kurtzman

aversion – platonic hatred
Jan Vercammen

aviation – proof that, given the will, we have the capacity to achieve the impossible
Eddie Rickenbacker

awards – the badges of mediocrity
Charles Ives
– a measurement of the degree to which an Establishment meets the talent which it had hindered and helped
Norman Mailer
– something like haemorrhoids; in the end every asshole gets one
Frederic Raphael

b

baby – *pl.* the enemies of the human race
Isaac Asimov
– a small creature that gets you down during the day and up at night
Jasmine Birtles
– a loud noise at one end and no sense of responsibility at the other
Ronald Knox
– something you carry inside you for nine months, in your arms for three years and in your heart till the day you die
Monica Mason
– God's opinion that life should go on
Carl Sandburg

babysitter – someone you pay by the hour to eat all your food and let your kids do what they want
Jasmine Birtles

bachelor – a man who comes to work every morning from a different direction
Joey Adams
– a man who believes that opportunity is meant to be embraced, but not engaged
O A Battista
– a man who can take a nap on top of the bedspread
Milton Berle

– a man who has missed the opportunity to make some woman miserable
Jasmine Birtles
– a widower who never was married
Jacques Canut
– someone who thinks for a long time before saying 'No'
Maurice Chevalier
– an unaltered male
John S Crosbie
– unhappy misfit who blames his lack of commitment on the fact that his mother is not available
Cy DeBoer
– a man who takes marriage seriously
Michel Déon
– a man who lives like a king and dies like a beggar
L S Lowry
– one who knows more about women than a married man. If he didn't, he would be married too
H L Mencken
– a thing of beauty and a boy forever
Helen Rowland
– a man who never Mrs anybody
Thomas Stone
– a man who is married to himself
Jan Vercammen
– someone who would like to be married, but not all the time
Helen Vita
– a guy who leans toward women – but not far enough to lose his balance
Earl Wilson
– a man who never makes the same mistake once
Ed Wynn
(see also *unmarried man*)

bachelor of arts – one who makes love to a lot of women, and yet has the art to remain a bachelor
Helen Rowland

bachelorhood – one way of keeping all that alimony money for yourself
Gene Perret

bad taste – simply saying the truth before it should be said
Mel Brooks

bagel – a pretzel that got its head together
Ron Smith

bagpipes – the missing link between music and noise
E K Kruger

baker's dozen – twelve of today's doughnuts and one of yesterday's
Johnny Hart

baldness – the best protection against loss of hair
Markus M Ronner
– nudism on a higher level
Frank Sinatra

James Baldwin – Martin Luther Queen
Dorothy Dean

ball – man's most disastrous invention, not excluding the wheel
Robert Morley

ballet – the ectoplasm of music
Russell Green
– the fairies' baseball
Oscar Levant
– an opportunity for arms and legs to talk
Jan Schepens
(see also *chat-chat-chat, dance, lambada, tango*)

ballot box – a most inadequate mechanism of change
Maxim Drabon

bank – a place where they lend you an umbrella in fair weather and ask for it back when it begins to rain
Robert Frost
– a place that will lend you money if you can prove that you don't need it
Bob Hope
– a prestigious establishment that in the end will lend us our own money
Willy Reichert

banker – a pawnbroker with a manicure
Joey Adams

bankruptcy – a legal proceeding in which you put your money in your pants pocket and give your coat to your creditors
Joey Adams

barbecue – the plural of burning wounds
Johan Anthierens

– a suburban summer ritual at which the eldest male of the household presides over a burnt offering that's undercooked on the inside
Rick Bayan
– smoke without fire
Colin Bowles

barber – an authority on everything except how to cut hair properly
William H Roylance

bargain – something you can't use at a price you can't resist
Franklin P Adams

baritones – the born villains in opera
Leonard Warren

bartender – a splendid person who practices psychiatry on the cheap by keeping his mouth closed, his ears open, and the glass filled
Edmund H Volkart

baseball – cricket played with a strong American accent
George Mikes

basic research – what I am doing when I don't know what I am doing
Wernher von Braun
(see also *research*)

bathroom – where your child doesn't need to go until you're backing your car out of the driveway
Joyce Armor
(see also *flush toilet, lavatory*)

bathroom scale – something you step on in the morning, and all it does is make you angry
Milton Berle

bay – a huge expanse of water surrounded by restaurants and hotels
Alfredo La Mont

beach – a place where a woman goes today when she has nothing to wear
Milton Berle

Beaujolais – a nice wine that makes women happy when men drink it
Henry Clos-Jouve
(see also *wine*)

beautiful woman – one who loves me
Sloan Wilson
(see also *woman*)

beauty – the child of love
Havelock Ellis
– love in self-expression
Richard Roberts
– a fruit which we look at without trying to seize it
Simone Weil

bed – a terrifying place for a man who is not sure who he is
Jenny James
– the best place for reading, thinking, or doing nothing
Doris Lessing

beer – an intoxicating golden brew that re-emerges virtually unchanged an hour later
Rick Bayan
– grain of a higher grade
Henk Kooyman

behavioural psychology – the science of pulling habits out of rats
Douglas Bush
(see also *psychology*)

belcanto – power training for the vocal cords
Fernand Lambrecht

Belgium – a country invented by the British to annoy the French
Charles de Gaulle

belief – an idea that possesses the mind
Robert Bolton
– to confuse things with their names
Jean-Paul Sartre

belly – nothing more than a small container of excrement
Guido van Heulendonk

Tony Benn – the Bertie Wooster of Marxism
Malcolm Bradbury

Bergamasque – what you put over your face when you're eating a Wimpy
Denis Norden

best friend – the one who brings out the best in you
Henry Ford
(see also *friend, real friend, true friend*)

bestseller – what a book is called when as many people buy it in a year as fill a stadium for a single local rugby match
Rick Bayan
– a book on which the publisher earns a lot of money
Louis Paul Boon
– a book which somehow sells well simply because it is selling well
Daniel J Boorstin
– the gilded tomb of a mediocre talent
L P Smith
(see also *book, classic book*)

Beverly Hills – a pool's paradise
L L Levinson

bigamist – an Italian's description of his last visit to London
Johnny Hart

bigamy – the original time share concept
Cy DeBoer
– one way of avoiding the painful publicity of divorce and the expense of alimony
Oliver Herford
– the only crime on the books where two rites make a wrong
Bob Hope
– proof that one plus one can make three
Jan Schepens

big egos – big shields for lots of empty space
Diana Black
(see also *egoist, human ego*)

big sisters – the crabgrass in the lawn of life
Charles M Schulz

biographer – an artist upon oath
Desmond MacCarthy

biography – history seen through the prism of a person
Louis Fischer
– a region bounded on the north by history, on the south by fiction, on the east by obituary, and on the west by tedium
Philip Guedalla

– voyeurism embellished with footnotes
Robert Skidelsky
– to give a man some kind of shape after his death
Virginia Woolf

birth control – a way of avoiding the issue
Jasmine Birtles

birthday – an annual reminder that the more you slow down, the more time accelerates
Edmund H Volkart

bisexuality – doubles your chances for a date on Saturday night
Woody Allen

bitch – underdog
Piet Grijs

bitterness – indigestion of the heart
Colin Bowles

blackbirds – the cellos of the deep farms
Anne Stevenson

blank verse – a device for making poetry easier to read and harder to write
H L Mencken
– poetry written without rhyme, often without reason
Edmund H Volkart
(see also *good poem, literature, poem, poetry*)

block grant – a solid mass of money surrounded on all sides by governors
Ross K Baker

blood – a red liquid material often found in the alcohol streams of certain individuals
Leonard Rossiter

blue jeans – trousers that should be worn by farm girls milking cows
Yves Saint Laurent

blush – a weakness of youth and an accomplishment of experience
Oliver Herford

boast – always a cry of despair, except in the young it is a cry of hope
Bernard Berenson

Bolivians – barely metamorphosed llamas, who have learned to talk but not to think
José Merino

Bolshevism – Czarism in overalls
George Jean Nathan
(see also *communism, Russian communism*)

bombs – firework to the sleepy
Norman Mailer

bombshell – the exclusion of a cricketer from a team
J B Morton

bon mots – the words other people wish they had said
Jean Cocteau

book – *pl.* literary works that entertained children before television was invented
Joyce Armor
– *pl.* the compasses and telescopes and sextants and charts which other men have prepared to help us navigate the dangerous seas of human life
Jesse Lee Bennett
– the blessed chloroform of the mind
Robert Chambers
– mostly better than the film
Gaston Durnez
– the world's most patient medium
Northrop Frye
– just trees with squiggles on them
Hammond Innes
– *pl.* a load of crap
Philip Larkin
– *pl.* what they make a movie out of for television
L L Levinson
– the death of a tree
Saint-John Perse
– *pl.* funny little portable pieces of thought
Susan Sontag
– the corpse of an idea
Eric van der Steen
– *pl.* lighthouses erected in the sea of time
Edwin Whipple
(see also *bestseller, classic book, literature, novel*)

bookie – a pickpocket who lets you use your own hands
Henry Morgan

book review – a brief but informative essay that spares readers the ordeal of digesting an actual book
Rick Bayan
(see also *criticism*)

book reviewer – *pl.* little old ladies of both sexes
John O'Hara
– a barker before the door of a publisher's circus
Austin O'Malley
(see also *critic, good critic, reviewmanship*)

boomerang – a piece of wood that is homesick
Patrick de Witte

bop – the shorthand of jazz, an epigram made by defying the platitude of conventional harmony
Kenneth Tynan
– the complex response of over-sensitive men to a world they are afraid would reject the natural expression of their emotions
Colin Wilson

borders – the scars of history
Emmanuel Berl

bore – the kind of a man who never knows how badly he feels until you ask him
O A Battista
– someone who persists in holding his own views after we have enlightened him with ours
Malcolm S Forbes
– a fellow who opens his mouth and puts his feats in it
Henry Ford
– a person who monopolizes the conversation talking about himself when you want to talk about yourself
Edward Jablonski & Lowell Thomas
– a man who when asked how he is, tells you
Bert Leston Taylor
– a fellow talker who can change the subject to his topic of conversation faster than you can change it back to yours
Laurence J Peter
– a man in love with another woman
Mary Pettibone Poole
– one who knows as well as you do what he is going to say next
Mignon McLaughlin

boredom – the most horrible of wolves
Jean Giono
– one face of death
Julien Green
– often the cause of promiscuity, and always its result
Mignon McLaughlin
– a form of criticism
William Phillips

boring – another word for a safe, undisturbed life
Dimitri Frenkel Frank

born executive – a guy whose father owns the business
Harvey Kurtzman
(see also *executive*)

borrower – a man who tries to live within your means
O A Battista

boss – a personal dictator appointed to those of us fortunate enough to live in free societies
Rick Bayan
– someone who is always on time only to see who isn't
Hans Söhnker
(see also *modern boss*)

Boston – a festering mud puddle
Ellis Arnall

bourgeois – an epithet which the riff-raff apply to what is respectable, and the aristocracy to what is decent
Anthony Hope

bourgeois morality – largely a system of making cheap virtues a cloak for expensive vices
George Bernard Shaw
(see also *morality*)

bowling – marbles for grown-ups
L L Levinson

boxing – a lot of white men watching two black men beat each other up
Muhammad Ali
– a mutual infliction of brain damage for the amusement of the public
Rick Bayan

– the only sport in the world where two guys get paid for doing something they'd be arrested for if they got drunk and did it for nothing
Carl Foreman
– the only racket where you're almost guaranteed to end up as a bum
Rocky Graziano
– the best and most individual lifestyle you can have in society without being a criminal
Randy Neumann

brain – my second favorite organ
Woody Allen
– a wonderful organ that starts working the moment you get up in the morning, and does not stop until you get into the office
Robert Frost

brainstorming – the privilege of people who cannot afford to think properly
Gerrit Komrij

bravery – the capacity to perform properly even when scared half to death
Omar Bradley
– being the only one who knows you're afraid
Franklin P Jones

bravo – a word with an exclamation mark included
Piet Grijs

break dancing – a recent, popular Terpsichorean invitation to visit a chiropractor
Edmund H Volkart

breakfast-time – the critical period in matrimony
A P Herbert

breath – air no one else wanted anymore
Piet Grijs

brevity – the soul of lingerie
Dorothy Parker

brick – the most efficient remote control
Patrick de Witte

brilliant conversationalist – one who talks to you about yourself
Lisa Kirk

brilliant epigram – a solemn platitude gone to a masquerade ball
Lionel Strachey
(see also *epigram*)

Britain – the grit in the European oyster
John Major

broad-mindedness – the result of flattening high-mindedness out
George Santayana

Broadway – a branch of the narcotics world run by actors
Bertolt Brecht
– the hardened artery
Walter Winchell

Broadway musical – currently a circus without elephants of memorable tunes, aimed at impressionable out-of-towners who mistake garishness for entertainment, and grandiosity for talent
Rick Bayan
(see also *musical*)

brokee – someone who buys stock on the advice of a broker
Robert Barron & Jim Fisk

broker – a man who runs your fortune into a shoestring
Alexander Woollcott

budding astronaut – a young man who is determined to go far
O A Battista
(see also *astronaut*)

budget – just another name for a family quarrel
Milton Berle

builder's estimate – a sum of money equal to half the final cost
Neil Collins

building – a string of events belonging together
Chris Fawcett

bullfight – an abattoir in fancy dress
Colin Bowles

bullfighting – the only art in which the artist is in danger of death and in which the degree of brilliance in the performance is left to the fighter's honour
Ernest Hemingway

bureaucracy – nothing more than a hardening of an organization's arteries
William P Anthony
– a continuing congregation of people who must act more or less as one
J K Galbraith
– the antithesis of democracy
Jo Grimond
– the mask of modern fascism
Fernand Lambrecht
– the only form of human organization that can manage to pass a hot potato through a small crack
Norman Mailer
– the modern form of despotism
Mary McCarthy
– the art of making the possible impossible
Javier Pascual Salcedo

bureaucrat – a Democrat who holds some office that a Republican wants
Alben W Barkley
– *pl.* the only people in the world who can say absolutely nothing and mean it
Hugh Sidey

business – the art of extracting money from another man's pocket without resorting to violence
Max Amsterdam
– a combination of war and sport
André Maurois
– always an excuse for infidelity
Henry Root

businessman – one who gets the business and completes the transaction – all the rest are clerks and labourers
Kin Hubbard
– the only man who is forever apologizing for his occupation
H L Mencken
– someone who sells under the price, pays more taxes than he earns and invests the credit balance in real estate
Julien de Valckenaere

butler – a solemn procession of one
P G Wodehouse

C

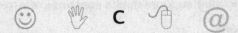

cable television – proof God is a man
Cy DeBoer
– a splendid addition to ordinary television in that it increases the choices among entirely interchangeable programs
Edmund H Volkart
(see also *television*)

cab drivers – living proof that practice does not make perfect
Howard Ogden
(see also *enterprising taxi driver, taxi*)

café – a failed restaurant
Colin Bowles

calendar – memento morning
Piet Grijs

Call me Ishmael – archaic novel opening, now updated to 'e-mail me Ishmael'
Mike Barfield

camel – animal made on the last day of Creation, with the leftovers
Simon Carmiggelt
– a horse designed by a committee
Alec Issigonis

camera – an instrument that teaches people how to see without a camera
Dorothea Lange

camera obscura – the one used in making most modern films
Edmund H Volkart

camp – a lie that tells the truth
Philip Core

California – a great place if you happen to be an orange
Fred Allen
– the west coast of Iowa
Joan Didion
– the only state in the union where you can fall asleep under a rose bush in full bloom and freeze to death
W C Fields

Canada – a country so square that even the female impersonators are women
Richard Brenner
– a collection of ten provinces with strong governments loosely connected by fear
Dave Broadfoot
– the boring second fiddle in the American symphony
Andrei Gromyko
– the vichyssoise of nations – it's cold, half French, and difficult to stir
Stuart Keate
– the only country in the world that knows how to live without an identity
Marshall McLuhan
– a country whose main exports are hockey players and cold fronts. [Its] main imports are baseball players and acid rain
Pierre Trudeau

Canadian – a person who knows how to make love in a canoe
Pierre Berton
– *pl.* Americans with no Disneyland
Margaret Mahy

canapés – dead things on toast
Jack Segal

Cannes – the city where you lie on the beach and stare at the stars – or vice versa
Rex Reed

cannibal – a guy who goes into a restaurant and orders the waiter
Jack Benny
(see also *converted cannibal*)

canon – a law that is fired with religion
Colin Bowles

capital – what is left over when the primary needs of society have been satisfied
Aldous Huxley

capitalism – the process whereby American girls turn into American women
Christopher Hampton
– the astounding belief that the most wickedest of men will do the most wickedest of things for the greatest good of everyone
John Maynard Keynes

capitalism

– the gentlemen's method of slavery
Kwame Nkrumah
– government of the busy by the bossy for the bully
Arthur Seldon
– the survival of the fattest
Paul Smith

capital punishment – either an affront to humanity or a potential parking place
Larry Brown
– our society's recognition of the sanctity of human life
Orrin Hatch

car – something you really need when looking for a parking space
Fons Jansen
– a secular sanctuary for the individual, his shrine to himself, his mobile Walden Pond
Edward McDonagh
– the caraspace, the protective and aggressive shell of urban and suburban man
Marshall McLuhan
– technical invention that improved the reflexes of pedestrians
Lothar Schmidt

cardiac – obsessed poker player
Ray Hand

career – a job that has gone on too long
Jeff MacNelly

career girl – a woman who goes out and earns a man's salary instead of staying home and taking it away from him
Joey Adams

careful driver – one who has just received a traffic ticket
O A Battista
– one who honks his horn when he goes through a red light
Henry Morgan
(see also *driver*)

caring husband – a man who is so interested in his wife's happiness that he'll hire a detective to find out who's responsible for it
Milton Berle
(see also *husband, ideal husband, married man*)

caress – a blow in the face to a masochist
Myriam Thijs

cash – a sort of window-fastener to keep Love from flying out
Oliver Herford
– the one gift everyone despises and no one turns down
Mignon McLaughlin

cashflow – the movement of money in and out of a business – an oxymoron
Bruce Boston

cashpoint – the sharp end of banking
Keith Miles

cat – a pygmy lion who loves mice, hates dogs, and patronizes human beings
Oliver Herford
– one hell of a nice animal, frequently mistaken for a meatloaf
B Kliban
– a waste of fur
Rita Rudner

caution – mother of all vices
Francis Blanche
– fear on tiptoe
Miguel Zamacois

CB – it may stand for Citizens' Band, but sometimes when you listen to it for a long time it stands for 'Constant Bore'
Ron Rich

cease fire – a mutually agreed upon time-out in the game of war, brief enough to prevent peace but long enough to permit reinforcements
Edmund H Volkart

celebrity – a person who works hard all his life to become known, then wears dark glasses to avoid being recognized
Fred Allen
– a person who appears to have no gainful employment other than appearing on quiz programmes billed as a celebrity
Russell Ash
– a person who is known for his well-known-ness
Daniel J Boorstin
– someone whose first name doesn't matter
Albert Camus
– a person known to many people he is glad he doesn't
H L Mencken
– *pl.* intellectual fast food
Lance Morrow

cemetery – a place where a lot of over-ambitious young men come to a dead stop
O A Battista

censor – someone who chews our meat for us and decides what we should spit out
Colin Bowles
– a self-appointed snoophound who sticks his nose in other people's business
Bennett Cerf
– a man who knows more than he thinks you ought to
Granville Hicks

censorship – that what feeds the dirty mind more than the four letter word itself
Dick Cavett
– publicity paid for by the government
Federico Fellini
– a legal corollary of public modesty
Jonathan Miller
– the weapon of the hypocrite
Adriaan de Roover
– the ultimate blasphemy
Michael Rubinstein
– society's lack of confidence in itself
Potter Stewart

centaur – a man with a horse where his pants ought to be
Milton Berle

chair – anti-gravity machine
Richard Feynman

champion – someone who gets up when he can't
Jack Dempsey

chance – perhaps the pseudonym of God when he does not wish to sign his work
Anatole France

character – the ability to win an argument by keeping your mouth shut
O A Battista
– what emerges from all the little things you were too busy to do yesterday, but did anyway
Mignon McLaughlin

– a strange blending of flinty strength and pliable warmth
Robert Shaffer
– doing what is right when no one is looking
J C Watts

charity – sex *before* he takes you out to dinner
Cy DeBoer
– the sterilized milk of human kindness
Oliver Herford
– giving someone the washing machine it wasn't worth having mended
Faith Hines
– the milk of human blindness
Tom Masson
– a good way of reminding God that if we can do it, He can
Mignon McLaughlin
– the alibi of the rich
Robert Sabatier
– the only thing that can persuade us to get rid of old clothes and shoes
Julien de Valckenaere

charity ball – a tax deductible dance
P J O'Rourke

charm – a way of getting the answer yes without asking a clear question
Albert Camus
– what remains when all the rest has vanished
Maurice Chevalier
– the power to effect work without employing brute force
Havelock Ellis
– the best method to colour your grey hair
Robert Lembke
– something people have until they know it
Ernst Schulz

charming woman – one who notices me
John Erskine
(see also *woman*)

chastity – the facile ability to keep the legs crossed
Colin Bowles
– the most unnatural of the sexual perversions
Aldous Huxley

chastity belt – a labour-saving device
Joyce Armor

chat-chat-chat – dance, performed by three French cats
Guy Bernaert
(see also *ballet, dance, lambada, tango*)

cheating – two wrong people doing the right thing
Milton Berle

cheese – the adult form of milk
Richard Condon
– milk's leap toward immortality
Clifton Fadiman

chef – any cook who swears in French
Henry Beard

chemistry – applied theology
Augustus Owsley Stanley

cherry tomato – a marvelous invention, producing as it does a satisfactorily explosive squish when bitten
Judith Martin

chess – as elaborate a waste of human intelligence as you can find outside an advertising agency
Raymond Chandler
– the movement of pieces eating one another
Marcel Duchamp
– a game where the most intense mental activity leaves no traces
Man Ray
– a foolish expedient for making foolish people believe that they are doing something very clever when they are only wasting their time
George Bernard Shaw

chewing-gum – television for the teeth
Rick Bayan

chic – knowing which fingers to put in your mouth when you whistle for the waiter
Milton Berle

Chicago – a joint where the bulls and the foxes live well and the lambs wind up head-down from the hook
Nelson Algren
– a city where men are men and the police take VISA
Hugh Leonard
– a pompous Milwaukee
L L Levinson

chicken – walking layer of eggs inevitably on its way to the knife and fork
Simon Carmiggelt

chihuahua – a dog that looks like a dog that is still far away
Billiam Coronel

child – *pl.* nature's very own form of birth control
Dave Barry
– a drain on resources and your resources down the drain
Jasmine Birtles
– *pl.* the only future the human race has
William Saroyan
– *pl.* the only form of immortality that we can be sure of
Peter Ustinov
(see also *kids*)

childhood – a time of life that becomes shorter and shorter
Lea Couzin
– the country that produces the most nostalgic, contentious and opinionated exiles
Richard Eder
– a stage on which time and space become entangled
Yukio Mishima
– Last Chance Gulch for happiness. After that you know too much
Tom Stoppard
– the kingdom where nobody dies
Edna St. Vincent Millay
– a forgotten journey
Jean de la Varende
– that wonderful time of life when all you need to do to lose weight is to take a bath
Richard S Zera

childish game – one in which your wife beats you
Don Epperson

chimpanzee – God's first draft of a politician
Colin Bowles

Chinese food – poetry in little cups
Marc Callewaert

chiropractor – a slipped disc jockey
Milton Berle

chivalry – the courteous exterior of a bigot
Max Eastman
– an age-old protection racket which depends for its existence on rape
Susan Griffin
– going about releasing beautiful maidens from other men's castles, and taking them to your own castle
Henry W Nevinson

Christ – an anarchist who succeeded
André Malraux

christian – a man who feels repentance on Sunday for what he did on Saturday and is going to do on Monday
Thomas R Ybarra

Christianity – a great idea that's never been tried
Alex Ayres
– the world's monumental fraud if there be no future life
Martin J Scott
– the most materialistic of all great religions
William Temple

christian theology – the grandmother of Bolshevism
Oswald Spengler

christmas – the time of year kids get toys their fathers can play with
Milton Berle
– a holiday that persecutes the lonely, the frayed and the rejected
Jimmy Cannon
– a three-day festival dedicated to the birth of Bing Crosby
Willis Hall & Bob Monkhouse
– that time of year when people descend into the bunker of the family
Byron Rogers

church – a place in which gentlemen who have never been to heaven brag about it to people who will never get there
H L Mencken
– the only co-operative society that exists for the benefit of non-members
William Temple
– a hospital for sinners, not a museum for saints
Abigail van Buren

chutzpa – that quality enshrined in a man who, having killed his mother and father, throws himself on the mercy of the court as an orphan
Leo Rosten

cigarettes – killers that travel in packs
Mary Ott

cinema – the art of showing nothing
Claude Bresson
– death in action
Jean Cocteau
– the most beautiful fraud in the world
– truth twenty-four times a second
Jean-Luc Godard
(see also *cult film, film, Hollywood, movie*)

city – a place where everyone mutinies but no one deserts
Harry Hershfield
– a human zoo
Desmond Morris
– a natural territory for the psychopaths with histrionic gifts
Jonathan Raban
(see also *modern city*)

civilization – an attitude of equal respect for all men
Jane Addams
– the distance man has placed between himself and his excreta
Brian Aldiss
– the evolution from being a dirty man in a clean world to a clean man in a dirty world
Jacques Embrechts
– to install an Eskimo into a warm house so that he must work in order to buy a refrigerator
Gabriël Laub
– a perishable commodity
Helen MacInnes
– the attempt to reduce force to being the last resort
José Ortega Y Gasset
– the progress toward a society of privacy. The savage's whole existence is public, ruled by the laws of his tribe. Civilization is the process of setting man free from men
Ayn Rand
– a tear that flows back into the eye
Willem M Roggeman
– the intelligent management of human emotions
Jim Rohn
– that wouldn't be a bad idea
Albert Schweitzer
– a race between education and catastrophe
H G Wells

civil servants – men who write minutes, make professional assessments, who are never attacked face to face, who dwell in the Sargasso Sea of the Civil Service and who love the seaweed that conceals them
William Connor

classical music – music written by famous dead foreigners
Arlene Heath
– the kind that we keep hoping will turn into a tune
Kin Hubbard
(see also *music*)

classic book – a book that has never finished saying what it has to say
Italo Calvino
– a book that makes you sick in class
Karel Jonckheere
(see also *book*, *bestseller*)

cleaving – an activity which should be left to snails for cleaning ponds and aquariums
Janice Rule

Cleveland – two Hobokens back to back
Joan Holman

cliché – a metaphor that knew better times
Jan Boerstoel
– something well said in the first place
Bill Granger

climate – the weather in a foreign country
Colin Bowles

clone – a cell mate
Angie Papadakis

clothes – masks of the body
Jan G Elburg
– nudity in its most refined form
Jan Schepens

clown – a poet in action
Henry Miller

clubs – places where men spend all their time thinking angrily about nothing
Valentine Browne Castlerosse

clue – what the police find when they fail to arrest a criminal
J B Morton

coalition – the most intimate form of enmity
Lothar Schmidt

coarse drinker – a man who blames his hangover on the tonic water and not the gin
Michael Green

coarse golfer – one who has to shout 'fore' before he putts
Michael Green

co-author – the one who did most of the writing, receives the least praise and most of the criticism
Edmund H Volkart
(see also *author, writer*)

cocaine – God's way of saying you're making too much money
Robin Williams

cocktail party – the worst invention since castor oil
Elsa Maxwell
– a device for paying off obligations to people you don't want to invite to dinner
Charles Merrill Smith
– a place where you talk with a person you don't know about a subject you have no interest in
Lin Yutang

coexistence – what the farmer does with the turkey – until Thanksgiving
Mike Connolly

coffee – the drug of the intellectual
Hugo Raes
(see also *English coffee, Irish coffee*)

coincidence – the sum of unknown laws
Emile Borel
– the tenth muse
Enrique Jardiel Poncela

coincidence

– the window to another world
Harry Mulisch
– secret guest who enters without knocking
Antoon Vloemans

coitus – occasion to call on the gods of the clan. It is a sacred act, pure, absolute, bringing invisible forces into action
Frantz Fanon
(see also *making love, sex*)

collaboration – the process whereby two people create something each thinks is his own
Frank A Clark

college – a place where you have to go in order to find out that there's nothing in it
Kin Hubbard
– a fountain of knowledge where students come to drink
Bruce W van Roy

collision – what happens when two motorists go after the same pedestrian
Bob Newhart

colorado beetle – insect that is still angry at us because we ate his potato
Piet Grijs

comedy – tragedy interrupted
Alan Ayckbourn
– tragedy plus time
Carol Burnett
– 90 per cent perspiration and 10 per cent agents' fees
Wayne Cotter
– an unnatural act, like sodomy
Marty Feldman
– an ability to observe and see what's funny in a situation and be able to forget yourself enough to do it
Madeline Kahn
– a man in trouble
Jerry Lewis
– the very last alternative to despair
Frank Marcus
– the art of making people laugh without making them puke
Steve Martin
– society protecting itself – with a smile
J B Priestley

– the last refuge of the nonconformist mind
Gilbert Seldes
– a funny way of being serious
Peter Ustinov
– often only a farce by a deceased dramatist
Arthur Wing Pinero
– the kindly contemplation of the incongruous
P G Wodehouse
(see also *musical comedy, stand-up comedy*)

comedians – the second oldest profession which, like the first, has been ruined by amateurs
Ben Wariss

comics – famously tragic people
Marlon Brando

command – in computer science, a statement presented by a human and accepted by a computer in such a manner as to make the human feel as if he is in control
Anon
– getting people to go the way you want them to go – enthusiastically
William Westmoreland

commercial – the message of the media
Alice Embree
– *pl.* the last things in life you can count on for a happy ending
Robert Morley

commercialism – doing well that which should not be done at all
Gore Vidal

commercial television – the only sedative you take with your eyes
Vittorio de Sica
– the kind which, like a prostitute, tries to convince the customer that it's a business doing pleasure, or the reverse
Edmund H Volkart
(see also *television*)

committee – a group of people who individually can do nothing but as a group decide that nothing can be done
Fred Allen
– a group that keeps the minutes and loses hours
Milton Berle
– an animal with four back legs
John le Carré

– a thing which takes hours to put into minutes what can be done in seconds
Judy Castrina
– a cul-de-sac down which ideas are lured and then quietly strangled
Barnett Cocks
– a group of the unwilling, picked from the unfit, to do the unnecessary
Richard Harkness
– a small group of the unqualified appointed by the unthinking to undertake the utterly unnecessary
Fibber McGee

commonplaces – the tramways of intellectual transportation
José Ortega Y Gasset

common sense – perhaps the most equally divided, but surely the most underemployed, talent in the world
Christiane Collange
– the collection of prejudices acquired by the age of eighteen
Albert Einstein

communication – the ability to affect other people with words
Jim Rohn
(see also *effective communication*)

communism – the most painful path between capitalism and capitalism
Scott Adams
– the opiate of the intellectuals
Clare Booth Luce
– one big phone company
Lenny Bruce
– the opiate of the asses
John S Crosbie
– the enemy of free men
Robert H Hinckley
– a race in which all competitors come in first with no prizes
Kenneth Inchcape
– one-third practice and two-thirds explanation
Will Rogers
– the corruption of a dream of justice
Adlai Stevenson
(see also *Bolshevism, Russian communism*)

communist – a person who has given up all hope of becoming a capitalist
Joey Adams

– one who has nothing and wishes to share it with the world
Clement Attlee
– a socialist without a sense of humor
George Cutten
– a socialist in a violent hurry
G W Gough
– a person who publicly airs his dirty Lenin
Jack Pomeroy
– *pl.* people who fancied that they had an unhappy childhood
Gertrude Stein

commuter – *pl.* people who get there slowly but surly
Martin Baker
– one who spends his life
In riding to and from his wife;
A man who shaves and takes a train,
and then rides back to shave again.
E B White

compassion – the virtue of the prostitute
Francis Picabia
– a luxury of the affluent
Tony Randall
– the worst enemy of love
Jan Wolkers

compliment – the triumph of courtesy over honesty
Ralph Boller
– *pl.* things you say to people when you don't know what else to say
Constance Jones
– a friendly truth with a little make-up
Hannelore Schroth
– the applause that refreshes
John W Wierlein

composer – someone who connects heaven with earth by threads of music
Alan Hovhaness
– *pl.* a breed of men and women concerned with the arrangement of the same seven notes
Richard Rodgers

compromise – the art of dividing a cake so that everybody believes he or she got the biggest piece
Ludwig Erhard
– simply changing the question to fit the answer
Merrit Malloy

compromise

– the most honest way to dissatisfy both parties
Alexander Pola

compulsion – a highbrow term for a temptation we're not trying too hard to resist
Hugh Allen

computer – *pl.* the high-tech machines that enable first graders to make their parents feel like morons
Joyce Armor
– the fastest idiot invented so far
Steven de Batselier
– something like an Old Testament God, with a lot of rules and no mercy
Joseph Campbell
– *pl.* mirrors in which we admire our minds and forget our souls
Alan Harris

computer dating – a terrific experience if you're a computer
Rita Mae Brown

computer error – human error in operating a computer
Russell Ash

computer literacy – ability to move words on a screen without ever appreciating their capacity to move minds
Rick Bayan

computer literate – synonym for between 2 and 18 years of age
Mike Barfield

conceit – God's gift to little men
Bruce Barton

concentration – the ability to do your son's homework while he is watching television
Terry McCormick

concert – the overture to a collective fit of coughing
J Goudsblom
– a polite form of self-imposed torture
Henry Miller

conclusion – *pl.* usually consolidated guesses
Henry S Haskins
– the place where you got tired of thinking
Robert Matz

condominium – just an apartment with a down payment
Robert D Specht

condos – apartments with nice doors
Silver Rose

Coney Island – where the surf is one-third water and two-thirds people
John Steinbeck

conference – just an admission that you want somebody to join you in your troubles
Will Rogers
– most interesting before, between and after the speeches
Jan Schepens

confession – telling tales on yourself
Fons Jansen

confidence – that quiet assured feeling you have before you fall flat on your face
L Binder

conformist – someone who is too lazy to think and too tired to get up
Colin Bowles

conformity – the jailer of freedom and the enemy of growth
John F Kennedy

confusion – always the most honest response
Marty Indik
– a word we have invented for an order which is not understood
Henry Miller

Congress – these, for the most part, illiterate hacks whose fancy vests are spotted with gravy and whose speeches, hypocritical, unctuous and slovenly, are spotted also with the gravy of political patronage
Mary McCarthy

congressman – *pl.* the finest body of men money can buy
Morey Amsterdam
– a man who doesn't know where he's going, and he wants us to follow him
Milton Berle

conjugal bedroom – the coexistence of brutality and martyrdom
Karl Kraus

conscience – the perfect interpreter of life
Karl Barth
– memory, attention and anticipation
Henri Bergson
– the mother of sin
Georges Braque
– what your mother told you before you were six years old
Brock Chisholm
– the internal perception of the rejection of a particular wish operating within us
Sigmund Freud
– a small, still voice that makes minority reports
Franklin P Jones
– what hurts when everything else feels so good
Harvey Kurtzman
– the one thing that doesn't abide by majority rule
Harper Lee
– a mother-in-law whose visit never ends
H L Mencken
– a barking dog that doesn't bite
Alexander Pola
– the still small voice that makes you feel still smaller
James A Sanaker
– the quiet voice that warns you not to leave any fingerprints
Alberto Sordi
– that quiet voice which whispers that someone is watching
Julian Tuwim
– the best invention after language
Antoon Vloemans
(see also *good conscience, guilty conscience*)

consciousness – that annoying time in between naps
Peter Darbo
– the phenomenon whereby the universe's very existence is made known
Roger Penrose

consensus – the security blanket of the insecure
Pierre A Rinfret
– the negation of leadership
Margaret Thatcher

conservation – a state of harmony between men and land
Aldo Leopold
– humanity caring for the future
Nancy Newhall

conservation area – a place where you can't build a garage but you can build a motorway
James Gladstone

conservationists – people who pour trouble on oiled waters
Joel Rothman

conservatism – the politics of reality
William F Buckley Jr
– the worship of dead revolutions
Clinton Rossiter
– the maintenance of conventions already in force
Thorsten Veblen

conservative – a fellow who is standing athwart history yelling 'Stop!'
William F Buckley Jr
– someone who wants to keep what he already had lost
Gaston Durnez
– someone with a sense of tradition
Jan Eijkelboom
– someone who demands a square deal for the rich
David Frost
– a man who is too cowardly to fight and too fat to run
Elbert Hubbard
– a liberal, too old for ideals
Theo Mestrum
– a man who wants the rules changed so that no one can make a pile the way he did
Gregory Nunn
– a liberal who got mugged the night before
Frank Rizzo
– a man with two perfectly good legs who, however, has never learned to walk forward
Franklin D Roosevelt
– someone who believes in reform. But not now
Mort Sahl
– someone who looks at the past with optimism
Lévi Weemoedt
– someone who believes that nothing should be done for the first time
Alfred Wiggam

consistency – what requires you to be as ignorant today as you were a year ago
Bernard Berenson
– the hobgoblin of little minds
Dorothy Parker

consistency

– the last refuge of the imaginative
George Steiner
– a paste jewel that only cheap men cherish
William Allen White

constipation – nature's way of making pregnant women practice pushing
Joyce Armor

constitutional law – a ship with a great deal of sail but a very shallow keel
Robert H Bork

consultant – someone who will take your watch off your wrist and tell you what time it is
David Owen

consultation – a meeting doctors have to pass the time while the patient dies
Colin Bowles

consumer – a shopper who is sore about something
Harold Coffin

contempt – the weapon of the weak and a defense against one's own despised and unwanted feelings
Alice Miller

contraceptive – a pill or gadget that enables a couple to savour the mirth without the birth
Rick Bayan

contract – an agreement to do something if nothing happens to prevent it
L L Levinson
– an agreement that is binding only on the weaker party
Frederick Sawyer

convention – the damnation of progress. If you go down just one corridor of thinking, you never get to see what's in the side rooms
Trevor Bayliss

conversation – a form of communication in which some men never stop to think and some women never think to stop
Peter Darbo
– the slowest form of human communication
Don Herold

– the enemy of good wine and food
Alfred Hitchcock
– being able to disagree and still continue the discussion
Dwight MacDonald
– anecdote tempered by interruption
Raymond Mortimer
– monologues delivered in the presence of a witness
Margaret Miller
– listening to yourself in the presence of others
Sidney Tremayne
(see also *art of conversation, good conversation*)

converted cannibal – one who, on Friday, eats only fishermen
Emily Lotney
(see also *cannibal*)

cooking – an act of love
Alain Chapel
– eatable art
Marcella Hazan

coolie – a quickie in the snow
Milton Berle

co-opt – baby talk for corrupt
John Leonard

corn – bacon after it has been processed by a pig
William D Hickman

corporal – a barking soldier
Bernard Seulsten

corpulence – the curse of the eating class
Gaby vanden Berghe

corpus delicti – a delicious body
Julian Tuwim

cosigner – a damn fool with a ballpoint pen
Milton Berle

cosmetics – the only reason to look in the mirror in the morning
Cy DeBoer

costs – amount required to bankrupt the acquitted
Miles Kington

cost-of-living index – a list of numbers which proves that high prices are not expensive
Richard Weiss

cough – something that you yourself can't help, but everybody else does on purpose just to torment you
Ogden Nash

counsel – advice with a price tag
L L Levinson

counter tenor – anyone who can count to ten
Denis Norden

counting – the religion of this generation, it is its hope and its salvation
Gertrude Stein

country – a piece of land surrounded on all sides by boundaries, usually unnatural
Joseph Heller

country music – three chords and the truth
Harlan Howard
(see also *music*)

courage – what it takes to pass a State Trooper even when you can keep within the speed limit
O A Battista
– the ladder on which all the other virtues mount
Clare Boothe Luce
– the price that life exacts for granting peace
Amelia Earhart
– grace under pressure
Ernest Hemingway
– not the absence of fear, but the concealing of it
Nelson Mandela
– the judgment that something else is more important than fear
Ambrose Redmoon
– being scared to death and saddling up anyway
John Wayne
– the art of being the only one who knows you're scared to death
Earl Wilson
– one step ahead of fear
Coleman Young

courtesy – the small currency of virtue
Charles Tschopp

courtroom – a place where Jesus Christ and Judas Iscariot would be equals, with the betting odds in favor of Judas
H L Mencken

courts – the last refuge of the unpersuasive
Stephen Chapman

cow – a machine that makes it possible for people to eat grass
John McNulty

coward – a man in whom the instinct of self-preservation acts normally
Soraya Esfandiari
– a hero with a wife, kids, and a mortgage
Marvin Kitman

cowardice – a lack of ability to suspend the functioning of the imagination
Ernest Hemingway

create – to think more efficiently
Pierre Reverdy
– one way to kill death
Romain Rolland

creation – to try to orchestrate the universe to understand what surrounds us. Even if, to accomplish that, we use all sorts of strategems which in the end prove completely incapable of staving off chaos
Peter Greenaway

creative work – one of life's greatest pleasures, and the only one we will gladly interrupt
Mignon McLaughlin

creativity – the power to connect the seemingly unconnected
William C F Plomer

creativity in science – the act of putting two and two together to make five
Arthur Koestler
(see also *science*)

creator – a comedian whose audience is afraid to laugh
H L Mencken

credit – a system of buying time with money you don't have
Joey Adams

– something a man gets in one department store which enables him to buy something else in another
O A Battista
– the only enduring testimonial to man's confidence in man
James Blish
– an expression of exaggerated optimism
Marc Callewaert

credit card – what you use after you learn money can't buy everything
Joey Adams
– *pl.* a great way of spending money you wish you had
Milton Berle
– a laminated loan shark
Andrew Waterfield

credit card holder – member of the debt set
Peter Darbo

credibility gap – what happens to the same news between the morning telecast and the evening paper
O A Battista

credulity – the neighbour of thoughtlessness
Gys Miedema

crick – the noise made by a Japanese camera
John S Crosbie

cricket – a tough and terrible, rough, unscrupulous game. No wonder our American friends do not like it
A P Herbert
– a game which the English, not being a spiritual people, have invented in order to give themselves some conception of Eternity
Lord Mancroft
– the only game where the major part of the team can just idle around and watch a few of their number do the work
George Mikes

crime – anything that a group in power chooses to prohibit
Freda Adler
– a left-handed form of human endeavour
W R Burnett
– something that is committed by the lower class and punished by the upper class
David Frost & Antony Jay
– a logical extension of the sort of behavior that is often considered perfectly respectable in legitimate business
Robert Rice

criminal – one who gets caught
Leonard Rossiter
– a person with predatory instincts who has not sufficient capital to form a corporation
Howard Scott

critic – a bundle of biases held loosely together by a sense of taste
Whitney Balliett
– *pl.* eunuchs at a gang-bang
George Burns
– *pl.* venomous serpents that delight in hissing
W B Daniel
– a man created to praise greater men than himself, but he is never able to find them
Richard le Gallienne
– *pl.* coroners literary
Ernest Hemingway
– a haunter of unquiet graves. He tries to evoke the presence of a living art, but usually succeeds only in disturbing the peace of the dead
M J C Hodgart
– a man who expects miracles
James Huneker
– one who goes along for deride
L L Levinson
– a creature without a spiritual home, and it is his point of honor never to seek one
Desmond MacCarthy
– a gent who reports his prejudices and his preferences in such English as he is aquipped with
Richard Maney
– a man who prefers the indolence of opinion to the trials of action
John Mason Brown
– a man who boasts he is hard to please, when nobody tries to please him
H L Mencken
– a gong at a railroad crossing clanging loudly and vainly as the train goes by
Christopher Morley
– *pl.* those who would send Hedda Gabler to the Marriage Guidance Council
John Osborne
– someone who's at his best when you're at your worst
Tony Pettito
– a legless man who teaches running
Channing Pollock
– *pl.* actors *manqué* – some more *manqué* than others
Brian Rix

– *pl.* pygmies with poison darts who live in the valley of the sleeping giants
Dagobert D Runes
– the policeman of Literature. The author asks him the way and ends up in prison
Robert Sabatier
– a very strange animal: open at the front and nothing at the rear
Kurt Schwitters
– a man who knows the way but can't drive the car
Kenneth Tynan
– *pl.* pigs at the pastry cart
John Updike
– a newspaperman, whose sweetheart ran away with an actor
Walter Winchell
– *pl.* inkstained wretches
Alexander Woollcott
(see also *art critics, book reviewer, drama critic, good critic, music critic, reviewmanship, TV critic*)

criticism – insults permitted by law
Jean-Louis Barrault
– the formal discourse of an amateur
R P Blackmur
– a big bite out of someone's back
Elia Kazan
– asserted superiority
Henry Manning
– prejudice made plausible
H L Mencken
– the window and chandelier of art
George Jean Nathan
– *pl.* misbegotten abortions
Ralph Vaughan Williams
(see also *book review, dramatic criticism*)

croquette – hash that has come to a head
Irvin S Cobb

cuisine – when things taste like what they are
Prue Leith

cult – not enough people to make a minority
Robert Altman
– dogmatism chasing a catechism
Colin Bowles
– a religion with no political power
Tom Wolfe

cult figure – a guy who hasn't got the musical ability to make it to the charts
John Cale

cult film – a movie seen about fifty times by about that many people
Rick Bayan
(see also *film*)

culture – the bedrock, the final wall, against which one leans one's back in a god-forsaken chaos
John Cowper Powys
– television programmes so boring that they cannot be classed as entertainment
Quentin Crisp
– to know a hundred words more than the others
Frédéric Dard
– what is left over after you forgot everything you learned
Selma Lagerlöf
–an order of sensory preferences
Marshal McLuhan
– what your butcher would have if he were a surgeon
Mary Pettibone Poole
– the first requisite and the final objective of all development
Leopold S Senghor
– an instrument wielded by professors to manufacture professors, who when their turn comes, will manufacture professors
Simone Weil
– the arts elevated to a set of beliefs
Tom Wolfe

culture shock – what happens when a traveller suddenly finds himself in a place where yes means no, where a 'fixed price' is negotiable, where to be kept waiting in an outer office is no cause for insult, where laughter may signify anger
Alvin Toffler

cupboard – a place for hanging things after you run out of doorknobs
Doug Larson

curiosity – the key to creativity
Akio Morita
– a willing, a proud, an eager confession of ignorance
S Leonard Rubinstein
– the first step to betrayal
Magdalena Samozwaniec
– the wick in the candle of learning
William A Ward

curse – a prayer of an agnostic
Georges Elgozy

curve – a straight line, but more human
Eric van der Steen
– the loveliest distance between two points
Mae West

customer – an object to be manipulated, not a concrete person whose aims the businessman is interested to satisfy
Erich Fromm

cyberpunk – the futuristic bandit of the information highway: a black-hatted gunslinger with a microchip on his shoulder and a modem in his holster
Rick Bayan

cynic – one who is prematurely disappointed in the future
Sidney J Harris
– a sentimentalist afraid of himself
Lambert Jeffries
– a man who, when he smells flowers, looks around for a coffin
H L Mencken
– a romanticist turned sour
Lewis Nkosi
– a person searching for an honest man, with a stolen lantern
Edgar A Shoaff
– a man who looks at the world with a monocle in his mind's eye
Carolyn Wells

cynicism – the mightiest weapon against sadness
Marc Andries
– the madness of wisdom
Bergen Evans
– a successful effort to see the world as it is
Jean Genet
– an unpleasant way of saying the truth
Lillian Hellman
– the armour of the idealist
Lambert Jeffries
– disappointed idealism
Harry Kemelman
– the intellectual cripple's substitute for intelligence
Russell Lynes
– the only deadly sin
Henry Louis Stimson
– humor in ill-health
H G Wells

d

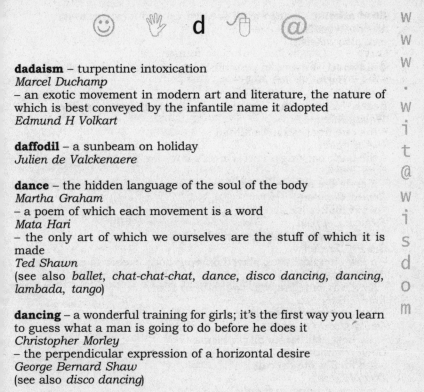

dadaism – turpentine intoxication
Marcel Duchamp
– an exotic movement in modern art and literature, the nature of which is best conveyed by the infantile name it adopted
Edmund H Volkart

daffodil – a sunbeam on holiday
Julien de Valckenaere

dance – the hidden language of the soul of the body
Martha Graham
– a poem of which each movement is a word
Mata Hari
– the only art of which we ourselves are the stuff of which it is made
Ted Shawn
(see also *ballet, chat-chat-chat, dance, disco dancing, dancing, lambada, tango*)

dancing – a wonderful training for girls; it's the first way you learn to guess what a man is going to do before he does it
Christopher Morley
– the perpendicular expression of a horizontal desire
George Bernard Shaw
(see also *disco dancing*)

dandruff – hair pollution
Joel Rothman

darling – the popular form of address used in speaking to a member of the opposite sex whose name you cannot at the moment recall
Oliver Herford

dates – the raisins of history
Jan Kott

daydreams – the gaseous decomposition of true purpose
Henry S Haskins

daytime TV – a plot by corporations to punish workers for staying home
Linda Rae Stowell
(see also *television*)

dead atheist – someone all dressed up and nowhere to go
Woody Woodbury
(see also *atheist*)

deadwood – anyone in your office who is more senior than you are
Robert Barron & Jim Fisk

death – a wonderful way of cutting down on your expenses
Woody Allen
– the one final exam we all fail
O A Battista
– the dark backing a mirror needs if we are to see anything
Saul Bellow
– merely the silence in the theatre when the last word is spoken
Remco Campert
– what makes life an event
Francis Coppola
– nature's way of telling us to slow down
Severn Darden
– a low chemical trick played on everybody except sequoia trees
J C Furnas
– life's way of telling you you've been fired
Rainer Geis
– the most convenient time to tax rich people
David Lloyd George
– the best solution to all problems
Georg Hermann
– the final wake-up call
Doug Horton
– to stop sinning suddenly
Elbert Hubbard
– the only thing we haven't succeeded in completely vulgarizing
Aldous Huxley
– the first condition of immortality
Stanislaw Jerzy Lec
– the only truth
Juan Ramòn Jiménez
– the anaesthetic from which none come round
Philip Larkin
– switching channels on TV
John Lennon
– but a new birth of the spirit into the great unknown
Pritish Nandy
– the scion of the house of hope
Dorothy Parker
– the only grammatically correct full-stop
Brian Patten

– one way of putting an end to all that junk mail
– a way of saying: Yesterday was the last day of the rest of your life
Gene Perret
– just a distant rumor to the young
Andy Rooney
– the penultimate commercial transaction finalized by probate
Bernard Rosenberg
– the price paid by life for an enhancement of the complexity of a live organism's structure
Arnold Toynbee
– a riddle with the solution on the other side
Geert van Beek
– a breathtaking event
Gaby vanden Berghe
– God's only defence againt human beings
Kees Versteeg
– nature's way of saying, 'Your table is ready'
Robin Williams
(see also *die, dying*)

debut – the first time a young girl is seen drunk in public
F Scott Fitzgerald

decency – an even more exhausting state to maintain than its opposite
Quentin Crisp

decent man – someone who is ashamed of the government he lives under
H L Mencken

deceptions – the oil to the wheels of life
Sidney Tremayne

decision – what a man makes when he can't find anybody to serve on a committee
Fletcher Knebel

décolletage – the only place men want depth in a woman
Zsa Zsa Gabor

decolonization – the replacing of a certain 'species' of men by another 'species' of men
Frantz Fanon

deficit – when adults tell the government what they want, and their kids end up paying for it
Richard Lamm

delay – the deadliest form of denial
C Northcote Parkinson

delicatessen – shop selling the worst parts of animals more expensively than the nice bits
Mike Barfield

demagogue – one who preaches doctrines he knows to be untrue to men he knows to be idiots
H L Mencken
– someone who speaks against the wind he made himself
Helmut Qualtinger

democracy – government by discussion, only effective if you can stop people talking
Clement Attlee
– system in which you say what you like and do what you are told
Gerald Barry
– the right for the lice to eat the lions
Philippe Berthelot
– organized distrust
Jan Blokker
– an abuse of statistics
Jorge Luis Borges
– 50 per cent of the bastards plus one
Philippe Bouvard
– the worst form of government except all the others that have been tried
Winston Churchill
– choosing your dictators, after they've told you what you think it is you want to hear
Alan Coren
– that form of government where everybody gets what the majority deserves
James Dale Davidson
– a collectivity of individuals
Ralph Waldo Ellison
– the name we give to the people when we need them
Robert de Flers
– the wholesome and pure air without which a socialist public organization cannot live a full-blooded life
Mikhail Gorbachov
– everyone should have an equal opportunity to obstruct everybody else
Celia Green
– a form of government by popular ignorance
Kin Hubbard

– the theory that the common people know what they want and deserve to get it good and hard
H L Mencken
– humanity chooses hopefully its executioners
Theo Mestrum
– hypocrisy without limitation
Iskander Mirza
– finding proximate solutions to insoluble problems
Reinhold Niebuhr
– a system of self-determination, the right to make the wrong choice
John Patrick
– a school with endless classes, permanent education
Shimon Peres
– a process by which the people are free to choose the man who will get the blame
Laurence J Peter
– an institution in which the whole is equal to the scum of the parts
Keith Preston
– self-control of the people
Barend Rijdes
– a form of government you have to keep for four years no matter what it does
Will Rogers
– a form of government that substitutes election by the incompetent many for appointment by the corrupt few
– a device that insures we shall be governed no better than we deserve
George Bernard Shaw
– a form of government in which it is permitted to wonder aloud what the country could do under first-class management
W H Soaper
– to give every voter a chance to do something stupid
Art Spander
– the recurrent suspicion that more than half of the people are right more than half of the time
E B White

democratic society – one in which the majority is always prepared to put down a revolutionary minority
Walter Lippmann

denial – how an optimist keeps from becoming a pessimist
Rick Bayan

dentist – someone who noses around in your mouth
Huguette de Backer

dentist's waiting room – a smartly furnished chamber of horrors
Shelley Berman

deodorants – commercial products that can't conceal the malodorousness of the programs they sponsor
Edmund H Volkart

descriptive passage – the dull part in a novel, thankfully lost in the TV adaptation
Mike Barfield

desert – a region that's constantly in need of a flood transfusion
– the best place to move if you can't save for a rainy day
Joel Rothman

desertion – the poor man's method of divorce
Arthur Hays

design – what the designer has when time and money run out
James Poole

designer – the sole human interface
Luc van Malderen

desire – a question to which no one has an answer
Luis Cernuda

desk – a dangerous place from which to view the world
John Le Carré
– a wastebasket with drawers
Bruce W van Roy

despair – the price one pays for setting oneself an impossible aim
Graham Greene
– anger with no place to go
Mignon McLaughlin

desperation – a man who shaves before weighing himself on the bathroom scales
RE Dorsey

destiny – statistics by another name
J M Prince

detached garage – one of the few remaining reasons that forces some people to take a walk
O A Battista

detective novel – the art-for-art's-sake of yawning Philistinism
V S Pritchett
(see also *novel*)

detour – a straight road which turns on the charm
Albert Brie
– something that lengthens your mileage, diminishes your gas, and strengthens your vocabulary
Oliver Herford

Deus-ex-machina – God falling out of a plane
Guy Commerman

developing countries – countries that are inhabited by people that have learned to eat with their mouths shut in expectation of food to be sent to them by civilized nations
Ward Ruyslinck

devil – an optimist who thinks that he can make man worse than he already is
Karl Kraus
– Adam and Eve's revenge
Theo Mestrum

diamond – a chunk of coal that stuck to the job
B C Forbes
– *pl.* A Girl's Best Friend
Leo Robin
– the only kind of ice that keeps a girl warm
Elizabeth Taylor
– a lump of coal with a migraine
L P Whitney

diary – all penned-up emotions
Holly S Greer
– photography with a pencil
Wim Kan
– a book of letters that were never mailed
Hugo Raes
– a document useful to the person who keeps it, dull to the contemporary who reads it, invaluable to the student, centuries afterwards, who treasures it
Ellen Terry

diatribe – a statement made by someone else with which you disagree. If you agreed with it, it would be an eloquent masterpiece
Walter H Schramm

dictatorship – a country where they have taken the politics out of politics
Sam Himmell
– the most complete form of jealousy
Curzio Malaparte
– a regime in which people quote instead of speak
Ignazio Silone
– a place where public opinion can't even be expressed privately
Walter Winchell

dictionary – the only place where success comes before work
Vidal Sassoon
– the only non-fiction publication that requires neither an index or a table of contents
Edmund H Volkart

die *v.* – probably the greatest kick of all
Herman Delahaye
– to go into the Collective Unconscious, to lose oneself in order to be transformed into form, pure form
Herman Hesse
– a way to deal with your loneliness
Hugo Olaerts
(see also *death, dying*)

diet – the specific types and quantities of food that any given individual will start eating tomorrow, next week, or after the beginning of the New Year
Henry Beard
– *pl.* mainly food for thought
N Wylie Jones
(see also *reducing diet*)

dieter – one who wishes others wouldn't laugh at his expanse
Al Bernstein

difficulty – the honour of the problem
Robert Sabatier

dignity – the art of making yourself heard without boasting
O A Battista
– cover for idiots
Roger Delvaux
– weakness overcome
Lola Falana

dilettante – a product of where wealth and literature meet
Douglas Dunn

– a philanderer who seduces the several arts and deserts each in turn for another
Oliver Herford

dinner theatre – a way of positively guaranteeing that both food and theater will be amateur and mediocre, which means unthreatening and therefore desirable
Paul Fussell
(see also *theatre*)

diploma – a remembrance of things passed
Holly S Greer

diplomacy – a continuation of war by other means
Chou En Lai
– to do and say the nastiest thing in the nicest way
Isaac Goldberg
– lying in state
Oliver Herford
– the art of fishing tranquilly in troubled waters
J Christopher Herold
– the art of restraining power
Henry Kissinger
– a game of chess in which nations are checkmated
Karl Kraus
– the art of jumping into troubled
ater without making a splash
Art Linkletter
– war with peaceful means
Werner Mitsch
– the art of saying 'Nice doggie' until you can find a rock
Will Rogers
– the art of letting someone have your own way
Daniele Vare

diplomat – a guy who goes to a nudist colony, sees some women playing tennis, and asks the score
Milton Berle
– one who can tell a man he's open-minded when he means he has a hole in his head
Henry O Dormann
– a man who always remembers a woman's birthday but never remembers her age
Robert Frost
– someone who says out loud what he doesn't think
Giovanni Guareschi
– a fellow that lets you do all the talking while he gets what he wants

diplomat

Kin Hubbard
– someone who convinces his wife that a fur coat would make her look fat
Alfredo La Mont
– one who can cut his neighbour's throat without having his neighbour notice it
Trygve Lie
– a man who thinks twice before he says nothing
Frederick Sawyer
– a person who can tell you to go to hell in such a way that you actually look forward to the trip
Caskie Stinnett
– a head waiter who's allowed to sit down occasionally
Peter Ustinov
– *pl.* babies in silk hats playing with dynamite
Alexander Woollcott

dirt – the by-product of a systematic ordering and classification of matter
Mary Douglas

discipline – remembering what you want
David Campbell
– the bridge between goals and accomplishment
Jim Rohn
– the refining fire by which talent becomes ability
Roy L Smith

disc jockey – *pl.* the wriggling ponces of the spoken word
D G Bridson
– *pl.* electronic lice
Anthony Burgess– a person who refer
to Austral
a as being the flipside of the world
Robert Orben

disco dancing – dancing for people who hate dancing . . . There is no syncopation, just the steady thump of a giant moron knocking in an endless nail
Clive James
(see also *dancing*)

discontent – the beginning of intent
Mack Reynolds

discovery – seeing what everyone else has seen and thinking what no one else has thought
Albert Szent-Györgi

discretion – the polite word for hypocrisy
Christine Keeler
– to look when nobody notices
Fernand Lambrecht
– the talent some women have of knowing with whom they can be indiscreet
Sidney Tremayne
– to find it beyond [one's] dignity to look through a keyhole as long as there is a key in it
Joop van Breemen

Disneyland – purgatory, with better parking space
Herman le Compte

distributed system – one in which the failure of a computer you didn't even know existed can render your own computer unusable
Leslie Lamport

dividends – hush money to shareholders
Robert Barron & Jim Fisk

divorce – nature's way of recycling
Jasmine Birtles
– fission after fusion
Rita Mae Brown
– a game played by lawyers
Cary Grant
– a tragedy that after a while feels suspiciously like relief
Faith Hines
– a way of having your legs amputated and still keep the feeling in your toes
Gys Miedema
– the ideal medicine for a sick marriage, but it doesn't kill all the germs
Robert Sabatier
– the best way to replace the first mistake by a second
Jan Schepens
– from the Latin word meaning to rip out a man's genitals through his wallet
Robin Williams

divorcee – a woman who gets richer by decrees
John S Crosbie
– a secondhand book
Georges de Porto-Riche

doctor – the only man without a guaranteed cure for a cold
Dominic Cleary

– a man licensed to make grave mistakes
L L Levinson

doctorship – the art of getting one up on the patient without actually killing him
Stephen Potter

doctor's bill – the bitterest pill of all
Gust Gils

dog – the only friend you can buy for money
Joey Adams
– *pl.* sons of bitches
W C Fields
– a domesticated animal least smart about humans
Adolf Nowaczynski
– an indefatigable and unsavoury engine of pollution
John Sparrow

donation – a confession of guilt
Jan Greshoff

Don Juan – a tourist in a hurry
Maurice Donnay

donsmanship – the art of criticising without actually listening
Stephen Potter

doodling – the brooding of the hand
Saul Steinberg

door – a keyword
Johan Anthierens
– what a dog is perpetually on the wrong side of
Ogden Nash

drama – life with the dull bits cut out
Alfred Hitchcock
– what literature does at night
George Jean Nathan

drama critic – a person who surprises the playwright by informing him what he meant
Wilson Mizner
– a man who leaves no turn unstoned
George Bernard Shaw
(see also *critic, good critic, reviewmanship*)

dramatic criticism – venom from contented rattlesnakes
Percy Hammond
(see also *criticism*)

dramatist – ventriloquist of the soul
Stanislaw Jerzy Lec

drawing – a way of reasoning on paper
Saul Steinberg

dread – a remote infinity of possibility
Howard P Kainz, Jr

dream *v.* – the only luxury of the poor
Fritz Francken

dream *n.* – the memory of the night
Jeroen Brouwers
– but the ghost of a shadow
Joseph Devlin
– the theater where the dreamer is at once scene, actor, prompter, stage manager, author, audience, and critic
Carl Jung
– the bearer of a new possibility, the enlarged horizon, the great hope
Howard Thurman
– an image of truth
Jeanette Winterson

dress code – the unwritten law that teenagers must dress alike to assert their independence
Joyce Armor

driver – the most dangerous part of a car
Léo Campion
(see also *careful driver*)

drug – *pl.* a spiritual form of gambling
Norman Mailer
– that substance which, when injected into a rat, will produce a scientific report
Robert Matz
(see also *miracle drug*)

drunkenness – the failure of a man to control his thoughts
David Grayson
– temporary suicide
Bertrand Russell

Dublin – a city where you can see a sparrow fall to the ground, and God watching it
Conor Cruise O'Brien

duchy – the wife of a duke
Leo Rosten

duck – a bird that walks like it has been on horseback all day
Hans Ferrée

dullness – the first requisite of a good husband
W Somerset Maugham

dumbwaiter – one who asks if the kids would care to order dessert
Joyce Armor

dummy teat – silencer
Pelicano

Dutchmen – Englishmen that drive on the right
Louis Paul Boon
– bulldozers of justice
Hugo Claus
– Germans who think they are not Germans because they drink milk
Gerard Reve

Dutch treat – the major achievement of the women's movement in the nineteen-seventies
Nora Ephron

duty-free liquor – flying blind
Colin Bowles

duty free shopping – nothing less than Government-sponsored smuggling
Ross Benson

dying – one of the few things that can be done just as easily lying down
Woody Allen
(see also *death, die*)

dyspeptic – a man that can eat his cake and have it too
Austin O'Malley

e

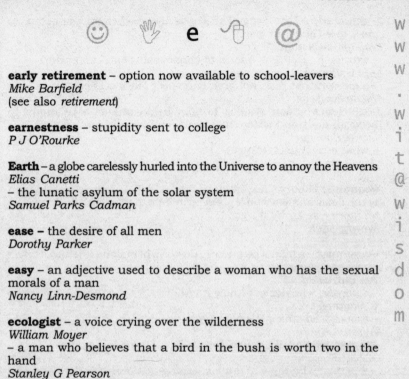

early retirement – option now available to school-leavers
Mike Barfield
(see also *retirement*)

earnestness – stupidity sent to college
P J O'Rourke

Earth – a globe carelessly hurled into the Universe to annoy the Heavens
Elias Canetti
– the lunatic asylum of the solar system
Samuel Parks Cadman

ease – the desire of all men
Dorothy Parker

easy – an adjective used to describe a woman who has the sexual morals of a man
Nancy Linn-Desmond

ecologist – a voice crying over the wilderness
William Moyer
– a man who believes that a bird in the bush is worth two in the hand
Stanley G Pearson
– someone who writes a 1,000 page book asking where have all the trees gone
Joel Rothman

ecology – the political substitute for the word 'mother'
Jesse Unruh

economic development – development of more intensive ways of exploiting the natural environment
Richard Wilkinson

economic independence – the foundation of the only sort of freedom worth a damn
H L Mencken

economics – the only field in which two people can share a Nobel Prize for saying opposing things
Roberto Alazar

– the study of the general methods by which men co-operate to meet their material needs
William Beveridge
– extremely useful as a form of employment for economists
J K Galbraith
– a subject that does not greatly respect one's wishes
Nikita Kruschev
– a science which studies human behaviour as a relationship between ends and scarce means which have alternative uses
Lionel Robbins
– what economists do
Jacob Viner

economic theory – a systematic application and critical evaluation of the basic analytic concepts of economic theory, with an emphasis on money and why it's good
Woody Allen

economist – a man who knows 100 ways of making love but doesn't know any women
Art Buchwald
– someone who doesn't know it either
C Buddingh'
– a man who states the obvious in terms of the incomprehensible
Alfred A Knopf
– a man who would marry Farrah Fawcett for her money
Robert Kolson
– a person who talks about something he doesn't understand and makes you feel you are ignorant
George Meany
– *pl.* people who earn their living by predicting that it will be hot in August, cold in January – but not necessarily
Robert Orben
– an expert who will know tomorrow why the things he predicted yesterday didn't happen today
Laurence J Peter
– someone who deals with figures but has too small a personality to become a bookkeeper
Robert Reich
– *pl.* the failed priests of our generation
Louis Rykeyser

economy – idealism in its most practical form
Calvin Coolidge
– the best cure for the national economy
Ashley Cooper

– going without something you do want, in case you should someday want something which you probably won't want
Anthony Hope
– cutting down other people's wages
J B Morton
– game in which A tries to take from B what he already took from C
Bernard Seulsten
(see also *planned economy*)

ecstasy – a drug so strong it makes white people think they can dance
Lenny Henry

editing – quarreling with writers
Harold Ross
– the most companionable form of education
Edward Weeks

editor – a person who knows precisely what he wants but isn't quite sure
Walter Davenport
– one who separates the wheat from the chaff and prints the chaff
Elbert Hubbard
(see also *great editor*)

education – something you get so you can work for guys with no education
Morey Amsterdam
– what parents receive when they sit in on a conversation between teenagers
Jasmine Birtles
– learning what you didn't even know you didn't know
Daniel J Boorstin
– the soul of a society as it passes from one generation to another
G K Chesterton
– a state-controlled manufactory of echoes
Norman Douglas
– the transmission of civilization
Ariel & Will Durant
– a progressive discovery of our own ignorance
Will Durant
– the process of casting false pearls before real swine
Irwin Edman
– the jewel casting brilliance into the future
Mari Evans
– helping the child realize his potentialities
Erich Fromm

– hanging around until you've caught on
Robert Frost
– the incalculation of the incomprehensible into the indifferent by the incompetent
John Maynard Keynes
– a method by which one acquires a higher grade of prejudices
Laurence J Peter
– the only human enterprise based on the confident anticipation of failure
R A Read
– one of the chief obstacles to intelligence and freedom of thought
Bertrand Russell
– what survived when what has been learnt has been forgotten
B F Skinner
– a leading out of what is already there in the pupil's soul
Muriel Spark

educational television – the bright gray blackboard
Henri Dieuzaide
(see also *television*)

effective communication – 20 per cent what you know and 80 per cent how you feel about what you know
Jim Rohn
(see also *effective communication*)

efficiency – intelligent laziness
David Dunham

efficiency expert – a guy who puts unbreakable glass on all the fire alarms
Milton Berle

egghead – one who stands firmly on both feet in mid air on both sides of an issue
Homer Ferguson

egoist – someone who cares more for himself than me
Julian Tuwim
(see also *big egos, human ego*)

egomaniac – a guy who thinks he's always right and he's wrong
Gene Perret
– a man who thinks that if he hadn't been born, people would have wondered why
Dan Post

egotism – the art of seeing in yourself what others cannot see
George Higgins
– the anaesthetic that dulls the pain of stupidity
Frank Leahy
– nature's compensation for mediocrity
L A Safian
– a case of mistaken nonentity
Barbara Stanwyck

Egypt – where the Israelites would still be if Moses had been a bureaucrat
Laurence J Peter

Eiffel Tower – Centrepoint after it has paid back taxes
Colin Bowles

election – *pl.* things that are held to see if the polls were right
Joey Adams
– a way of changing the cast of a political comedy, without affecting the performance
Edmund H Volkart

election year – the time politicians want to help us out of all the trouble they got us into in the first place
Gil Stern

electricity – the peril the wind sings to in the wires on a gray day
Janet Frame

electronic mail – a communications system with built-in delays and errors designed to emulate those of the postal service
Anon

elegance – good taste, *plus* a dash of daring
Carmel Snow

elegy – a posthumous ode
C Buddingh'

elephant – the only mammal that can masturbate and keep his hands free
François Cavanna
– a mouse built to government specifications
Robert Heinlein
– a square animal with a tail in front and behind
Cecil Hunt

eloquence – saying the proper thing and stopping
Stanley Link

e-mail – male form of headache. 'Darling, not now, I have to check my e-mail, go to bed!'
Leo de Haes

emancipated – a woman who behaves as badly as a man
Mike Barfield

empowered organization – one in which individuals have the knowledge, skill, desire, and opportunity to personally succeed in a way that leads to collective organizational success
Stephen R Covey

encyclopedia – a Latin term. It means to paraphrase a term paper
Greg Ray

enemy – someone you haven't seen for a while
Bob Ellis
– anybody who's going to get you killed, no matter which side he's on
Joseph Heller
– one who has his own best welfare at heart, not yours
Mignon McLaughlin

engineer – someone who can build for a dollar what any damn fool can build for ten
Robert A Heinlein

England – French colony that went in the wrong direction
Georges Clémenceau
– a country infested with people who love to tell us what to do, but who very rarely seem to know what's going on
Colin MacInnes
– the paradise of individuality, eccentricity, heresy, anomalies, hobbies, and humors
George Santayana
– a museum of style
Tom Wolfe

English – the perfect language to sell pigs in
Michael Hartnett
– a simple, yet hard language. It consists entirely of foreign words pronounced wrongly
Kurt Tucholsky

English Catholics – just Protestants, protesting against Protestantism
D H Lawrence

English coffee – just toasted milk
Christopher Fry
(see also *coffee, Irish coffee*)

Englishman – *pl.* probably the most tolerant, least religious people on earth
David Goldberg
– a man who lives on an island in the North Sea governed by Scotsmen
Philip Guedalla
– a creature who thinks he is being virtuous when he is only being uncomfortable
George Bernard Shaw

English novel – a story in which two people fall in love and then complain to each other for 400 pages
Colin Bowles
(see also *novel*)

enjoyment – the way to reduce discomfort
Theo Mestrum

enterprise – the hope of our future
Jim Rohn

enterprising taxi driver – one who starts his meter running the instant you wave him down
O A Battista
(see also *cab drivers, taxi*)

entrepreneur – a person who is willing to take risks for the sake of profits, like thieves or bank robbers
Edmund H Volkart

entrepreneurship – the last refuge of the troublemaking individual
James K Glassman

environment – everything that isn't me
Albert Einstein

environmentalist – someone concerned with the influence of affluence
Joel Rothman

envy – the basis of democracy
Bertrand Russell

enzymes – things invented by biologists that explain things which otherwise require harder thinking
Jerome Lettvin

epic – a movie with Charlton Heston in it
James Agate

epigone – someone looking for his own identity and finds someone else's
Sulamith Sparre

epigram – only a wisecrack that's played Carnegie Hall
Oscar Levant
– a half-truth so stated as to irritate the person who believes the other half
Shailer Mathews
(see also *brilliant epigram*)

epitaph – a belated advertisement for a line of goods that has been permanently discontinued
Irvin S Cobb

equality – the only true and central premise from which constructive ideas can radiate freely and be operated without prejudice
Mervyn Peake
– diminutive
Albert Willemetz

erosion – shore leave
Joel Rothman

eroticism – nothing more than a bit of mucus
Ingmar Bergman
– the hub around which the world is turning
Octavio Paz

error – a failure to adjust immediately from a preconception to an actuality
John Cage
– a mistake when we refuse to admit it
Marilyn vos Savant
(see also *mistake*)

escort – a prostitute with knowledge of the theatre
Mike Barfield

essay – a literary device for saying almost everything about almost anything
Aldous Huxley

essayist – a lucky person who has found a way to discourse without being interrupted
Charles Poore

eternal boredom – the price of constant vigilance
Marion J Levy

eternal love – eternity in its most transitory form
Hans Krailsheimer
(see also *art of love, fall in love, first love, ideal love, love, platonic love, true love*)

eternity – the second hour of Trivial Pursuit
Milton Berle
– two people and a roast turkey
James Dent
– another word for change
Gerald Gould
– period needed to fullfil all our desires
Julien de Valckenaere
– that endless amount of time one spends awaiting the arrival of the doctor or the tax refund
Edmund H Volkart

ethics – aesthetics from within
Pierre Reverdy

etiquette – getting sleepy in company and not showing it
Hyman Berson
– behaving yourself a little better than is absolutely essential
Will Cuppy

eunuch – a man who has had his works cut out for him
Robert Byrne

euthanasia – a way of putting old people out of their family's misery
Mike Barfield
– never having to tell your parents you're sorry
Jasmine Birtles

Eve – the better and revised edition of Adam
Helen Vita

evil – that which one believes of others. It is a sin to believe evil of others, but it is seldom a mistake
H L Mencken

exaggeration – a truth that has lost its temper
Kahlil Gibran

exasperation – the mind's way of spinning its wheels until patience restores traction
George L Griggs

exception – a new rule of the future
Roland Leune

exclamation mark – a question mark with an erection
Pierre Alechinsky
– the last straw of someone who cannot write
Jan Blokker
– the literary equivalent of a man holding up a card reading LAUGHTER to a studio audience
Miles Kington

exclusiveness – a characteristic of recent riches, high society, and the skunk
Austin O'Malley

excuses – the most profitless things to manufacture
B C Forbes
– the nails used to build a house of failure
Don Wilder

executive – an ulcer with authority
Fred Allen
– a person who always decides; sometimes he decides correctly, but he always decides
John H Patterson
(see also *born executive*)

exercise – a short cut to the cemetery
John Mortimer

exhibitionist – a naked man commonly arrested for standing in a window so that he might be glimpsed by a woman standing outside; when a naked *woman* is in the window and the man is standing outside, he is then arrested as a peeping tom
Rick Bayan
– someone who preferably hides himself in a shop-window
Gys Miedema

exhilaration – that feeling you get just after a great idea hits you, and before you realize what's wrong with it
Peter Darbo

existence – plagiarism
E M Cioran

– the precarious attainment of relevance in an intensely mobile flux of past, present and future
Susan Sontag
– knowing the difference between what I am now and what I was then
Alice Walker

existentialism – means that no one else can take a bath for you
Delmore Schwartz

exit – an entry somewhere else
Tom Stoppard

experience – what you have left after you have forgotten her name
John Barrymore
– the mother of science
Henry George Bohm
– a dim lamp, which only lights the one who bears it
Louis-Ferdinand Céline
– often a dreadful list of ghastly mistakes
J Chalmers Da Costa
– a physician who only comes when you are cured
Béatrix Dussane
– what allows us to repeat our mistakes, only with more finesse
Derwood Fischer
– what a man does with what happens to him
Aldous Huxley
– that marvelous thing that enables you recognize a mistake when you make it again
Franklin P Jones
– the one thing you have plenty of when you're too old to get the job
Laurence J Peter
– what you get when you don't get what you want
Dan Stanford
– a comb life gives you after you lose your hair
Judith Stern
– God's gift when you no longer need it
Jan Sztaudinger
– what remains after the pain
Piet Theys

expert – a lecturer from out of town, with slides
Jim Baumgarten
– a man who has made all the mistakes which can be made, in a very narrow field
Niels Bohr
– the man you're seated next to at a dinner party
Cy DeBoer

expert

– someone called in at the last minute to share the blame
Sam Ewing
– someone who knows some of the worst mistakes that can be made in his subject and how to avoid them
Werner Heisenberg
– a man who can explain very thoroughly why his prognosis was wrong
Jo Herbst
– a man who never makes small mistakes
Tom Phipps
– one who knows so much about so little that he neither can be contradicted, nor is worth contradicting
Henry Ward
– a mechanic away from home
Charles E Wilson
– a man who has stopped thinking
Frank Lloyd Wright
(see also *specialist*)

extravagance – anything you buy that is of no earthly use to your wife
Franklin P Adams
– the way the other fellow spends his money
T Harry Thompson

extremist – someone who does what he thinks God would do if He knew the facts
Marijke Höweler

f

face – the focus of an answer
Gys Miedema
– the soul of the body
Ludwig Wittgenstein

face-lift – temporary restoration of the visage we wore in youth, but one size smaller
Rick Bayan

acts – ventriloquists' dummies. Sitting on a wise man's knee they may be made to utter words of wisdom; elsewhere they say nothing, or talk nonsense
Aldous Huxley
– stupid things
Ronald Reagan

fags – the only people who are kind to wordly old women
Truman Capote

failure – the condiment that gives success its flavor
Truman Capote
– nature's plan to prepare you for great responsibilities
Napoleon Hill
– *pl.* finger posts on the road to achievement
Charles F Kettering
– a luxury not yet afforded to women
Susan Seidelman
– a highly contagious disease
Tennessee Williams
– another stepping-stone to greatness
Oprah Winfrey
– often the line of least persistence
Zig Ziglar

fairness – the opposite of passion
Kathleen Betsko

fair tax structure – one that allows everybody to cheat evenly
Milton Berle
(see also *income tax, taxes, wealth tax*)

faith – an illogical belief in the occurence of the improbable
H L Mencken
– believing in things when common sense tells you not to
George Seaton
– the flip side of fear
Susan L Taylor
– the state of being ultimately concerned
Paul Tillich

faithful woman – a woman who doesn't want two men to suffer at the same time
Jan Vercammen
(see also *woman*)

fall in love – to create a religion that has a fallible god
Jorge Luis Borges
(see also *art of love, eternal love, first love, ideal love, love, platonic love, true love*)

false modesty – the fear of being responsible for one's own talents
Theo Mestrum
(see also *modesty*)

fame – a happy combination of talent and timing
Colin Bowles
– being asked to sign your autograph on the back side of a cigarette packet
Billy Connolly
– apt to be what someone writes on your tombstone
Finlay Peter Dunne
– a powerful aphrodisiac
Graham Greene
– being known by more people than you know
Jonathan Miller
– being insulted by Groucho Marx
Denis O'Brien
– a flippant lover
Wole Soyinka
(see also *famous*)

familiarity – the opiate of the imagination
Arnold Toynbee

family – a group of people who each like different breakfast cereal
Milton Berle
– a court of justice which never shuts down for night and day
Malcolm de Chazal
– a group of individuals united by blood and arguing about money
Etienne Rey
– one of nature's masterpieces
George Santayana
– a dear octopus from whose tentacles we never quite escape
Dodie Smith
– the people most likely to give you the flu
Jane Wagner
(see also *good family*)

family planning – working out how to keep the children occupied for the whole weekend
Jasmine Birtles

family room – what the bathroom becomes as soon as one wishes to use it
Edmund H Volkart

family vacation – one where you arrive with five bags, four kids and seven I-thought-you-packed-its
Ivern Ball
(see also *good holiday, holiday, naturist holiday, vacation*)

famous – to be forgotten fifty years later than usual
Ite Boerema
– to be more quoted than read
Arno Sölter
(see also *fame*)

fanatic – someone who doubted and took a decision
Godfried Bomans
– someone who can't change his mind and who won't change the subject
Winston Churchill
– a man who does what he thinks the Lord would do, if He knew the facts of the case
Peter Finley Dunne
– a man who consciously overcompensates a secret doubt
Aldous Huxley
– one who sticks to his guns whether they're loaded or not
Franklin P Jones

fanaticism – the refuge of people without intellect
Mark Grammens
– spiritual chauvinism
Hans Kudszus
– redoubling your effort when you have forgotten your aim
George Santayana

fan club – a group of people who tell an actor he is not alone in the way he feels about himself
Jack Carson

farm – an irregular patch of nettles bounded by short-term notes, containing a fool and his wife who didn't know enough to stay in the city
S J Perelman

farmer – the only man in our economy who buys everything at retail, sells everything he sells at wholesale, and pays the freight both ways
John F Kennedy
– a handy man with a sense of hummus
E B White

fascism – the future refusing to be born
Aneurin Bevan
– capitalism in decay
Vladimir Lenin
– a counter-revolution against a revolution that never took place
Ignazio Silone

– capitalism plus murder
Upton Sinclair

fashion – what you adopt when you don't know who you are
Quentin Crisp
– a substitute for taste
R G Hawtrey
– a barricade behind which men hide their nothingness
Kin Hubbard
– something that goes in one year and out the other
Denise Klahn
– that which is unwearable until everyone else is wearing it, by which time it is unfashionable
Leonard Rossiter
– *pl.* induced epidemics
George Bernard Shaw
– finding something you're comfortable in and wearing it into the ground
Tuesday Weld

fashion designers – people who live off the fad of the land
Frank Tyger

fast food – food delivered promptly because it isn't worth waiting for
Mike Barfield
– the kind that nutritionists and slow eaters complain about, the former because it endangers health, the latter because of indigestion
Edmund H Volkart

fate – God's little nephew
Herman Brusselmans
– non-awareness
Jan Kott

fathead – one person who cannot be helped by a diet
O A Battista

father – a man with pictures in his wallet where his money used to be
Milton Berle

fatherhood – the greatest single preserve of the amateur
Jasmine Birtles
– pretending that the present you love is soap-on-a-rope
Bill Cosby

fatherly love – the ability to expect the best from your children, despite the facts
Jasmine Birtles

fatness – the curse of the eating class
Gaby vanden Berghe

fault – the name I give to my experiences
J Goudsblom

fax – a modern enhancement of the telephone, enabling us to send and receive illegible information in seconds; also ideal for communicating bad news without the inconvenience of having to talk to the person at the other end
Rick Bayan

fear – the seductive power of goodness
Bertolt Brecht
– the fire that melts Icarian wings
Florence E Coates
– that little darkroom where negatives are developed
Michael Pritchard
– a two-edged sword that sometimes cuts the wielder
Jackie Robinson
– a noose that binds until it strangles
Jean Toomer
– the father of courage and the mother of safety
Henry Hallam Tweedy

federal aid – a system of making money taken from the people look like a gift when handed back
Carl Workman

feet – incorrigible trouble makers
Robert Morley

feminism – the radical notion that women are people
Cheris Kramarae & Paula Treichler
– the result of a few ignorant and literal-minded women letting the cat out of the bag about which is the superior sex
P J O'Rourke

feminist – a woman of whom the mice are afraid
Fernand Lambrecht
(see also *anti-feminist*)

fertilizer shortage – the endangered faeces list
Joel Rothman

fervour – the weapon of choice of the impotent
Frantz Fanon

fiction – the most uncreative form of publishing
Paul Hamlyn
– a confidence trick trying to make people believe something is true that isn't
Angus Wilson

fidelity – not having more than one man in bed at the same time
Frederic Raphael
– a strong itch with a prohibition to scratch
Julian Tuwim

filing cabinet – a place where you can lose things systematically
T H Thompson

film – a machine for seeing more than meets the eye
Iris Barry
– a petrified fountain of thought
Jean Cocteau
– the world in an hour and a half
Jean-Luc Godard
– fairy tales for grown-ups
Sergio Leone
(see also *cinema, cult film, Hollywood, movie*)

film directors – people too short to become actors
Josh Greenfield

film-making – a kind of hysterical pregnancy
Richard Lester

final delusion – the belief that one has lost all delusions
Maurice Chapelan

finance – the art of passing currency from hand to hand until it finally disappears
Robert W Sarnoff
– large money resources, usually found in two places: the highworld and the underworld
Edmund H Volkart

financier – a pawnbroker with imagination
Arthur Wing Pinero

fire – the burning of objects not intended for burning
Tatyana Tolstaya

First Lady – the hardest unpaid job in the world
Pat Nixon

first love – a promise that will be kept by others
Senta Berger
(see also *art of love, eternal love, fall in love, ideal love, love, platonic love, true love*)

first-rate laboratory – one in which mediocre scientists can produce outstanding work
Patrick MS Blackett

first-time parents – people who are anxious for their child to start talking
Jasmine Birtles
(see also *parents*)

fish bone – posthumous revenge of the fish
Tristan Bernard

fishing – an excuse to drink in the daytime
Jimmy Cannon
– a delusion entirely surrounded by liars in old clothes
Don Marquis

flashlight – a great gadget for storing dead batteries
Milton Berle

flatterer – one who says things to your face that he wouldn't say behind your back
Henry Millington

flattery – the art of telling someone exactly what he thinks of himself
Harvey Kurtzman

flea – an insect which has gone to the dogs
Julian Tuwim

flirtation – merely an expression of considered desire coupled with an admission of its impracticability
Marya Mannes
– attention without intention
Max O'Rell
– the froth on top of the wine of love
Sidney Tremayne
– to be intimate from a distance
Hellmut Walters

flirting – the gentle art of making a man feel pleased with himself
Helen Rowland

floppy disc – serious curvature of the spine
Kris Brand

flush toilet – the basis of Western civilization
Alan Coult
(see also *bathroom, lavatory*)

flying – hours and hours of boredom sprinkled with a few seconds of sheer terror
Gregory 'Pappy' Boyington
(see also *art of flying*)

folk dance – originally, a way to kill wasps
Toon Verhoeven

folk singing – just a bunch of fat people
Bob Dylan

food – an important part of a balanced diet
Fran Lebowitz

football – a game designed to keep coalminers off the streets
Jimmy Breslin
(see also *professional football*)

footballers – miry gladiators whose sole purpose in life is to position a surrogate human head between two poles
Elizabeth Hogg

forecast – a pretence of knowing what would have happened if what does happen hadn't
Ralph Harris

forecasting – an important sense *backward*-looking, vividly compared to steering a ship by its wake
Ralph Harris

foreign aid – taxing poor people in rich countries for the benefit of rich people in poor countries
Bernard Rosenberg

foreign correspondent – someone who flies around from hotel to hotel and thinks that the most interesting thing about any story is

the fact that he has arrived to cover it
Tom Stoppard

foreigner – someone who doesn't understand cricket
Anthony Couch

foreign policy – an imitation of war by other means
Jean-François Revel

forgetting – a poor excuse for not remembering
J R DeBleyker

forgiveness – the key to action and freedom
Hannah Arendt
– a reflex for when you can't stand what you know
Jane Smiley
– a gift of high value. Yet its cost is nothing
Betty Smith

form – the balance between tension and relaxation
Ernest Toch

foundation – a large body of money completely surrounded by people who want some
Dwight MacDonald

fox – a wolf who sends flowers
Ruth Weston

frame – warning that the wallpaper is no art
Piet Grijs

France – a republic seasoned with garlic
Colin Bowles
– the only place where you can make love in the afternoon without people hammering on your door
Barbara Cartland
– a country divided into 60,000,000 Frenchmen
Pierre Daninos
– a country where the money falls apart and you can't tear the toilet paper
Billy Wilder

fraud – the homage that force pays to reason
Charles P Curtis

freedom – the fire which burns away illusion
James Baldwin
– when one hears the bell at 7 o'clock in the morning and knows it is the milkman and not the Gestapo
Georges Bidault
– nothing else but a chance to be better
Albert Camus
– an internal achievement rather than an external adjustment
Adam Clayton Powell Jr
– the oxygen of the soul
Moshe Dayan
– the right to be wrong, not the right to do wrong
John G Diefenbaker
– chaos, with better lighting
Alan Dean Foster
– just another word for nothing left to lose
Kris Kristofferson
– a bourgeois notion devised as a cloak for the spectre of economic slavery
Vladimir Lenin
– being able to choose whose slave I want to be
Jeanne Moreau
– a powerful animal that fights the barriers, and sometimes makes people wish for higher fences
Lance Morrow
– a short blanket that if it covers one part of the body, leaves some other part out in the cold
Guido Piovene
– the right to choose the habits that bind you
Renate Rubinstein
– a drunken whore
  Sprawling in a power maddened soldier's arms
Marina Tsvetayeva
– a food which must be carefully administered when people are too hungry for it
Lech Walesa

free enterprise – getting other people to do your work
Lewis Grizzard

freelance writer – one who gets paid by the word, per piece, or perhaps
Robert Benchley
– a tramp touting for odd jobs
Arnold Bennett
(see also *author, co-author, professional writer, screenwriter, writer*)

free press – 100 men imposing their prejudices on 100 million
Leo Rosten

free society – a society where it's safe to be unpopular
Adlai Stevenson

Frenchman – a German with good food
Fran Lebowitz
– an Italian with a bad temper
Dennis McEvoy

Freudian slip – when you say one thing but mean your mother
Anon

friend – someone who sees through you and still enjoys the view
Wilma Askinas
– someone who can read in your eyes
Herman Brusselmans
– someone who calls at your house even if he doesn't need anything
C Buddingh'
– someone with whom you dare to be yourself
Frank Crane
– *pl.* God's apology for relations
Hugh Kingsmill
– a man who has the same enemies you have
Stephen Leacock
– someone who makes me feel totally acceptable
Ene Riisna
– *pl.* people who borrow my books and set wet glasses on them
E A Robinson
(see also *best friend, real friend, true friend*)

friendship – a very taxing and arduous form of leisure activity
Mortimer Adler
– sharing the prejudice of experience
Charles Bukowski
– a common belief in the same fallacies, mountebanks and hobgoblins
H L Mencken
– tenderness without sex
Jeanne Moreau
– love at the first word
Harry Mulisch
– almost always the union of a part of one mind with a part of another; people are friends in spots
George Santayana
(see also *platonic friendship*)

frugality – being mean to yourself
L L Levinson

fuchsia – the world's most carefully spelled flower
Jimmy Barnes

fundamentalist – anyone who takes the Word of God too seriously
Rick Bayan

funeral eulogy – a belated plea for the defense delivered after the evidence is all in
Irvin S Cobb

future – the only kind of property that the masters willingly concede to slaves
Albert Camus
– the past in preparation
Pierre Dac
– a grown-up present
Franco Ferrucci
– something which everyone reaches at the rate of sixty minutes an hour
C S Lewis
– the dawn of the past
Teixeira de Pascoaes
– the paradise from which no one ever returned
Pierre Reverdy
– the past that turns around in its sleep
Eric van der Steen
– a race between education and catastrophe
H G Wells
– the past, entered through another gate
Arthur Wing Pinero

future shock – the shattering stress and disorientation that we induce in individuals by subjecting them to too much change in too short a time
Alvin Toffler

futurologist – a historian in reverse
Jules de Corte
– a job with a future
Kamagurka
– someone who looks back to the year 2500
Helmut Qualtinger

g

galaxy – five or six actresses
J B Morton

gambling – a way of getting nothing for something
Wilson Mizner
– the art of betting one's hard earned money in hopes of winning it back
Paula Stinnett

game show – how television sends us the message that greed is cute
Rick Bayan
(see also *televsion*)

garbage – the waste that civilization finds easy to produce, difficult to collect, and all but impossible to dispose of
Edmund H Volkart

garden – a thing of beauty and a job forever
Joey Adams

garlic bread – bread travelling in bad company
Denison Flamingo

Charles de Gaulle – someone who looked like a female llama surprised in her bath
Winston Churchill

gelatine – a pain in the aspic
Henry Beard

genealogy – tracing yourself back to people better than you are
John Garland Pollard Jr

General – someone who risks *your* life for *his* country
Gerrit Komrij
– a Colonel who once was a soldier
Marc van Halsendaele

general opinion – the opinion of one or a few for which the public is held responsible
Muhammad Hijazi

genitals – a great distraction to scholarship
Malcolm Bradbury

genius – the intellectual shortage of one century, compensated by one man
Bertus Aafjes
– the talent for seeing things straight
Maude Adams
– one who shoots at something no one else can see, and hits it
Anon
– the power to be a boy again at will
James Barrie
– the capacity for productive reaction against one's training
Bernard Berenson
– a nephew who can do everything but make a living
Milton Berle
– a man who has two great ideas
Jacob Bronowski
– the ability to reduce the complicated to the simple
CW Ceram
– that superior alchemy that changes the vices of nature into the elements of destiny
Pierre Emmanuel
– another word for magic, and the whole point of magic is that it is inexplicable
Margot Fonteyn
– an infinite capacity for giving pains
Don Herold
– a man who can rewrap a new shirt and not have any pins left over
Dino Levi
– perseverence in disguise
Mike Newlin
– talent provided with ideals
William Somerset Maugham
– a little boy chasing a butterfly up a mountain
John Steinbeck
– a person so locked in one area of thought that he is consumed by it
Herman W Watts

genocide – the substitute for conversion
Dick Gregory

gentiles – people who eat mayonnaise for no reason
Robin Williams

gentility – what is left over from rich ancestors after the money is gone
John Ciardi

gentleman – a man who wouldn't hit a woman with his hat on
Fred Allen

– a man who understands women, but acts as though he doesn't
O A Battista
– someone who also writes poetry but keeps quiet about it
Louis Paul Boon
– a man who knows how to play the accordion, but doesn't
Al Cohn
– a man who uses a butter knife when dining alone
W F Dettle
– a man who never hurts anybody else unintentionally
Herbert Farjeon
– a contradiction in terms
Cheris Kramarae & Paula A Treichler
– someone who gives his seat in the bus to an ugly woman
Fernand Lambrecht
– one who never strikes a woman without provocation
H L Mencken
– a patient wolf
Henrietta Tiarks
(see also *man*)

German – a barking language
Frédéric Dard
– a language which was developed solely to afford the speaker the opportunity to spit at strangers under the guise of polite conversation
P J O'Rourke
– the most extravagantly ugly language, like someone using a sick-bag on a 747
William Rushton

Germany – a headquarters for constipation
George Grosz
– the only country where pop-singers look just like their songs
André Heller

gesticulation – any movement made by a foreigner
J B Morton

gift – a synonym of trade
Austin O'Malley

gifted – a word used by critics to describe an author or performer they find too promising to disparage, and too disappointing to promote
Edmund H Volkart

gift shop – a place where you can see all the things you hope your friends won't send you for Christmas
Jack Woolsey

gigolo – a fee-male
Isaac Goldberg

girl – a woman without a past
Marc van Halsendaele

glamour – what makes a man ask for your telephone number and a woman for the name of your dressmaker
Lilly Daché

glass – a well-dressed matchmaker between wine and tongue
Julien Vandiest

glory – one of the forms of human indifference
Valéry-Larbaud

glossary – shoeshine stand
Ray Hand

glutton – an abominable stow man
Shelly Friedman

gluttony – an emotional escape, a sign something is eating us
Peter de Vries
– not a secret vice
Orson Welles

goal – dream with a deadline
Diana Scharp Hunt
pl. – dreams we convert to plans and take action to fulfil
Zig Ziglar

God – a luxury I can't afford
Woody Allen
– the Celebrity-Author of the World's Best-Seller
Daniel J Boorstin
– the perfect dictator, because he does not exist
Remco Campert
– a satanic invention
Georges Elgozy
– dog spelled backwards
Paul McCartney

– the contrapuntal genius of human fate
Vladimir Nabokov
– a rumour
Dennis Potter
– the only reality
Gerard Reve
– the dumping ground of our dreams
Jean Rostand
– a living doll
Jane Russell
– the loneliness of mankind
Jean-Paul Sartre
– a book that you must read when closed
Cees van Dongen

gold rush – what happens when a line of chorus girls spot a man with a bank roll
Mae West

golf – an awkward set of bodily contortions designed to produce a graceful result
Tommy Armour
– a game whose aim is to hit a very small ball into an even smaller hole, with weapons singularly ill-designed for the purpose
Winston Churchill
– a game in which a ball one and a half inches in diameter is placed on a ball 8,000 miles in diameter. The object is to hit the small ball but not the larger
John Cunningham
– the loneliest of all games, not excluding postal chess
Peter Dobereiner
– a game with the soul of a 1956 Rotarian
Bill Mandel
– hockey at the halt
Arthur Marshall
– the best game in the world at which to be bad
A A Milne
– the most fun you can have without taking your clothes off
Chi Chi Rodriguez
(see also *handicapped golfer*)

good executive – a man who isn't afraid to correct a mistake made by his secretary – no matter how pretty she is
O A Battista

good behaviour – the last refuge of mediocrity
Henry S Haskins

The Good Book – one of the most remarkable euphemisms ever coined
Ashley Montagu

good conscience – the best make-up
Arletty
(see also *conscience, guilty conscience*)

good conversation – a poor substitute for good food
Robert Lynd
(see also *art of conversation, conversation*)

good conversationalist – not one who remembers what was said, but says what someone wants to remember
John Mason Brown

good critic – he who relates the adventures of his soul among masterpieces
Anatole France
– the sorcerer who makes some hidden spring gush forth unexpectedly under our feet
François Mauriac
(see also *art critics, book reviewer, critic, drama critic, music critic, reviewmanship, TV critic*)

good family – one that used to be better
Cleveland Amory
(see also *family*)

good holiday – one spent among people whose notions of time are vaguer than yours
J B Priestley
(see also *holiday, naturist holiday, vacation*)

good journalist – a kind of cross between Galahad and William Randolph Hearst
I F Stone
(see also *investigating journalist, journalist, rock journalism*)

good listener – a good talker with a sore throat
Katharine Whitehorn

good loser – a person who can stick to a diet
O A Battista
(see also *loser*)

good luck – a lazy man's estimate of a worker's success
Peter Darbo
(see also *luck*)

good marriage – the union of two forgivers
Ruth Graham
– at least 80 per cent good luck in finding the right person at the right time. The rest is trust
Nanette Newman
(see also *happy marriage, marriage*)

good memory – one trained to forget the trivial
Clifton Fadiman
(see also *memory*)

good music – that which penetrates the ear with facility and quits the memory with difficulty
Thomas Beecham
(see also *music*)

goodness – easier to give than to define
W H Auden

good newspaper – a nation talking to itself
Arthur Miller
(see also *newspaper*)

good old days – period when our ancestors had a very difficult time
C Buddingh'

good person – somebody who does good, but usually not very well
Alex Ayres

good poem – a musical painting full of ideas
Fernando Pessoa
(see also *literature, poem, poetry*)

good politician – quite as unthinkable as an honest burglar
H L Mencken
(see also *politician*)

good speaker – one who gets more applause when he is finished than when he is introduced
O A Battista

good storyteller – a person who has a good memory and hopes the other people haven't
Irving S Cobb

good taste – the enemy of creativity
Pablo Picasso

– the worst vice ever invented
Edith Sitwell
– the ability to keep saying *no*
Piet Theys

good teaching – one-fourth preparation and three-fourths theater
Gail Godwin
(see also *art of teaching, teaching*)

good women – hidden treasures who are only safe because nobody looks for them
Dorothy Parker

gorgonzola – the corpse of a dead cheese
Colin Bowles

gossip *v.* – the new pornography
Woody Allen
– that which no one claims to like – but everybody enjoys
Joseph Conrad
– a second language for women
Cy DeBoer
– a dishonest way of praising ourselves
Will Durant
– the opiate of the oppressed
Erica Jong
– what you say about the objects of flattery when they aren't present
P J O'Rourke
– to hear something you like about someone you don't
Earl Wilson
– the art of saying nothing in a way that leaves practically nothing unsaid
Walter Winchell

gossip *n.* – a person who creates the smoke in which other people assume there's fire
Dan Bennett
– a wither report
Raymond J Cvikota
– *pl.* people who have only one relation in common – God
Christopher Morley
– ear pollution
Joel Rothman
– just news running ahead of itself in a red satin dress
Liz Smith

gossip columnist – Judas with a notebook
Colin Bowles

– *pl.* the spies of life
Doris Dolphin
– *pl.* diseases, like flu. Everyone is subject to them
James Goldsmith
– a writer of both faked and friction
Colin M Jarman

gourmand – serious eater whose culinary opinions carry at least as much weight as he does
Henry Beard

gourmet – a glutton who reads French
Colin Bowles
– a glutton with a tux
Milton Berle
– a glutton with a dictionary
Millôr Fernandes
– a glutton with brains
Philip W Haberman Jr

govern – to choose how the revenue raised from taxes is spent
Gore Vidal

government – a kind of legalized pillage
Kin Hubbard
– the best paid theatre company
Hugo Olaerts
– the only vessel known to leak from the top
James Reston
(see also *ideal government*)

government bureau – the nearest thing to eternal life that we'll ever see on this earth
Ronald Reagan

grandchildren – the flashbacks of your children
Kris Jan Jacobs

Grand Old Man – anyone with snow-white hair who has kept out of jail till eighty
Stephen Leacock

grass widow – the angel a man loved, the human being he married, and the devil he divorced
Helen Rowland
(see also *widow*)

gratitude – not a formal feature of political life
David Patrick Kilmuir
– the most exquisite form of courtesy
Jacques Martain
– a sickness suffered by the dogs
Joseph Stalin

gray hair – God's graffiti
Bill Cosby

Grease – a movie of such grubbiness that after seeing it I felt like washing my skull out with soap
Clive James

great editor – a man of outstanding talent who owns 51 per cent of his newspaper's stock
Henry Watterson
(see also *editor*)

great literature – simply language charged with meaning to the utmost possible degree
Ezra Pound
(see also *literature, today's literature*)

great restaurants – mouth-brothels
Frederic Raphael
(see also *restaurant*)

great scandal – the public version of a great secret
Sidney Tremayne
(see also *scandal*)

great society – a place where the meaning of a man's life matches the marvels of man's labour
Lyndon B Johnson
(see also *society*)

greed – a weed that will harden your garden
Alan Harris
– weakness that cripples
Bettye J Parker-Smith

Greek tragedy – the sort of drama where one character says to another, 'If you don't kill mother, I will'
Spyros Skouras
(see also *tragedy*)

grin – the striptease of the smile
Paul Rodenko

growing old – being increasingly penalized for a crime you haven't committed
Anthony Powell
– a bad habit which a busy man has no time to form
André Maurois
(see also *age, old age*)

grown-up – a child with layers on
Woody Harrelson

grumbling – the death of love
Marlène Dietrich

guillotine – a French chopping centre
John S Crosbie

guilt – the price we pay willingly for doing what we are going to do anyway
Isabelle Holland

guilty conscience – the mother of invention
Carolyn Wells
(see also *conscience, good conscience*)

gun – the ambience of our society
Mark Medoff

h

habit – the chloroform of love
the cement that unites married couples
getting stuck in the mud of daily routine
the fog that masks the most beautiful scenery
the end of everything.
Geneviève Antoine-Dariaux
– a great deadener
Samuel Beckett
– something you can do without thinking – which is why most of us have so many of them
Frank A Clark
– a shirt made of iron
Harold Helfer

– the fingerprint of the character
Alfred Polgar
– a passion that suffers from amnesia
Julien Vandiest

hair – the bane of most women's lives
Joan Collins
– the only one real cure for baldness
Gene Perret

haircut – a metaphysical operation
Julio Cortâzar

halo – only one more thing to keep clean
Christopher Fry

Hamlet – the Mona Lisa of literature
T S Eliot
– the tragedy of tackling a family problem too soon after college
Tom Masson

hand – the cutting edge of the mind
Jacob Bronowski

handicapped golfer – anybody who plays with his boss
Milton Berle
(see also *golf*)

hangover – the wrath of the grapes
Anon

Hansard – history's ear, already listening
Herbert Samuel

happiness – grief that takes a short rest
Brigitte Bardot
– to be able to eat a pancake without having toothache
Belcampo
– what we really can see when it's over
Godfried Bomans
– having no notion of time
Stef Bos
– a by-product of an effort to make someone else happy
Gretta Brooker Palmer
– having a large, loving, caring, close-knit family in another city
George Burns

– a by-product of function. You are happy when you are functioning
William Burroughs
– a full-time job
Simon Carmiggelt
– a change of sorrows
Colette
– a delicate balance between what one is and what one has
F H Denison
– the only thing you can give without having
Henry O Dormann
– the sublime moment when you get out of your corsets at night
Joyce Grenfell
– watching TV at your girlfriend's house during a power failure
Bob Hope
– a warm bed pan
Christopher Hudson
– the full use of your powers along lines of excellence
John F Kennedy
– a second that wants to be an eternity
Gerrit Komrij
– a dull meal, with the dessert at the beginning
Pierre Lamure
– the interval between periods of unhappiness
Don Marquis
– a yesterday thing
Spike Milligan
– having a scratch for every itch
Ogden Nash
– a half-way station between too little and too much
Channing Pollock
– the quiet lull between problems
Paul Reiser
– the art of learning how to get joy from your substance
Jim Rohn
– to know one's limits and to cherish them
Romain Rolland
– wanting what you have
Hyman Schachtel
– nothing more than good health and a bad memory
Albert Schweitzer
– an imaginary condition, formerly attributed by the living to the dead, now usually attributed by adults to children, and by children to adults
Thomas Szasz
– what we throw overboard all the time in order to be able to fish for it
Julien de Valckenaere

happy life – one spent in learning, earning and yearning
Lillian Gish
(see also *life*)

happy marriage – a long conversation that always seems too short
André Maurois
(see also *good marriage, marriage*)

hara-kiri – Japanese for Cesarean Section
Cy DeBoer

hardware – the part of the computer that can be kicked
Jeff Pesis

harem – a floor show with a husband
Milton Berle

harp – a nude piano
Tom Horgan
– an over-sized cheese-slicer with cultural pretentions
Denis Norden

harpsicord – musical instrument that sounds like two skeletons copulating on a corrugated tin roof
Thomas Beecham
– a performance on a bird-cage with a toasting fork
Percy A Scholes
– musical instrument that sounds just like the ticking of a sewing machine
Ralph Vaughan Williams

haste – the enemy of politeness
Drusilla Beyfus

hate – a clash between our spirit and someone else's body
Cesare Pavese
– the coward's revenge for being humiliated
George Bernard Shaw

hatred – love frustrated
Ashley Montagu

hay fever – the real Flower Power
L L Levinson

health – having the same diseases as one's neighbours
Quentin Crisp

– what my friends are always drinking to before they fall down
Phyllis Diller
– the thing that makes you feel that now is the best time of the year
Franklin Pearce Adams

health food – any food whose flavor is indistinguishable from that of the package in which it is sold
Henry Beard

heart – the organ of fire
Michael Ondaatje

heart surgeon – highly qualified plumber
A G Brom

heavy metal – the idiot-bastard spawn of rock
Tim Holmes
– the transformation of precious jewels and gold into lead
Charles Shaar Murray

hell – the red-light district of Heaven
Fernand Auwera
– a place where no one believes in a solution any more
Ingmar Bergman
– to love no more
Georges Bernanos
– locked up for life in a Turkish prison with a Dutch cook
Jean Blaute
– when you get what you think you want
Anthony Clare
– New York city with all the escape hatches sealed
James T Frakes
– a half-filled auditorium
Robert Frost
– to wait without hope
André Giroux
– the devil's paradise
Robert Sabatier
– a place where the motorists are French, the policemen are German, and the cooks are English
Bill Sadgarden
– other people
Jean-Paul Sartre
– the Venus de Milo with anal eczema
Pol Vanhaverbeke

Audrey Hepburn – a walking x-ray
Billy Wilder

heredity – a splendid phenomenon that relieves us of responsibility for our shortcomings
Doug Larson
– what sets the parents of a teenager wondering about each other
Laurence J Peter

heresy – another word for freedom of thought
Graham Greene

hero – someone who rises above his own human weakness, for an hour, a day, a year, to do something
Betty DeRamus
– *pl.* men who glorify a life which they can't bear any longer
Jean Giraudoux
– someone who has been imprudent and unpunished
W F Hermans
– a man who would argue with the Gods, and so awakens devils to contest his vision
Norman Mailer
– the shortest-lived profession on earth
Will Rogers
– a man who does what he can
Romain Rolland
– someone who didn't know better, or didn't know at all
Wim Triesthof

hesitate – to give fate time to be ahead of our decisions
Julien de Valckenaere

heterosexuality – a boring and horrible lifestyle
Edith Massey

heterosexuals – the ungrateful children of gay culture
Harvey Fierstein

hibernation – a covert preparation for a more overt action
Ralph Waldo Ellison

hick town – one in which there is no place to go where you shouldn't be
Alexander Woollcott

highbrow – person who reads a novel before it is adapted for television
Mike Barfield

– the kind of person who looks at a sausage and thinks of Picasso
A P Herbert
– a person educated beyond his intelligence
Brander Matthews
– a man who has found something more interesting than women
Edgar Wallace

high heels – the impresario of women's legs
Paul Rodenko

high official – a person who can stay away from his office without being missed
Marc Callewaert

high school – the place where the band practices
Robert Maynard Hutchins

hip – the sophistication of the wise primitive in a giant jungle
Norman Mailer

historian – someone who wasn't there either
Frithiof Brandt
– someone who can predict the past and the present
F Hellers
– often only a journalist facing backwards
Karl Kraus
– an unsuccessful novelist
H L Mencken

historical words – words spoken by the great after their death
André Prévot

history – the sum total of the things that could have been avoided
Konrad Adenauer
– an art which must not neglect the known facts
Bernard Berenson
– the present, seen through the future
Godfried Bomans
– the sum total of man's successive rebellions
Albert Camus
– a vast early warning system
Norman Cousins
– the record of an encounter between character and circumstance
Donald Creighton
– an endless repetition of the wrong way of living
Lawrence Durrell

history

– an argument without end
Pieter Geyl
– an absurd happening into which more or less gifted people attempt to introduce some perspectives
Günter Grass
– a nightmare from which I am trying to awake
James Joyce
– the suprahuman force of an omnipotent society
Milan Kundera
– the short trudge from Adam to atom
L L Levinson
– the true myth of man's fall made manifest in time
Henry Miller
– the same play, performed by different actors
Henry de Montherlant
– the setting up, through the ages, of works which are consistently devoted to solving death and to overcoming it in the future
Boris Pasternak
– that little sewer where man loves to wallow
Francis Ponge
– the study of man's unhappiness
Raymond Queneau
– the category of human phenomena which tends to catastrophe
Jules Romains
– a nearly defunct field of study that is of value only to the extent that it glorifies everything previously debased, and vice versa
Bernard Rosenberg
– a bucket of ashes
Carl Sandburg
– the ship carrying living memories to the future
Stephen Spender
– the unfolding of miscalculation
Barbara Tuchman
– the science of that which doesn't happen twice
Paul Valéry
(see also *human history, political history*)

hobby – dummy for grown-ups
Julien de Valckenaere

hockey – a war in which people keep score
Milton Berle
– football with crutches
Piet Grijs
– a game played by six good players and the home team
Jim Murray

– a game where you take a stick and hit either the puck, or anyone who has touched the puck
Gene Perret
(see also *ice hockey*)

holding – the plural of building
Steven de Batselier

holding company – a thing where you hand an accomplice the goods while the policeman searches you
Will Rogers

hole – nothing at all, but you can break your neck in it
Austin O'Malley

holiday – short period between plans and memories
Lea Couzin
– a period of activity so intense that it can only be undertaken three or four weeks in the year
Miles Kington
– *pl.* an expensive trial of strength. The only satisfaction comes from survival
Jonathan Miller
(see also *good holiday, naturist holiday, vacation*)

Holland – a low-lying country full of low, lying people whose main object in life is to deceive the English by holding *Dutch auctions*, displaying *Dutch courage*, and talking *Double-Dutch*
W C Sellar & R J Yeatman

Hollywood – a place where people from Iowa mistake each other for stars
Fred Allen
– the only place in the world where an amicable divorce means each one gets fifty per cent of the publicity
Lauren Bacall
– a city in the US where someone is more likely to ask you Who's Whose than Who's Who
O A Battista
– a place where you can make an entire career out of baloney
Warren Beatty
– a cultural boneyard
Marlon Brando
– the only place where you can fail upwards
John G Dunne
– a mining camp in lotus land
F Scott Fitzgerald

hollywood

– the only place where you can wake up in the morning and hear the birds coughing in the trees
Joe Frisco
– an emotional Detroit
Lillian Gish
– the most beautiful slave-quarters in the world
Moss Hart
– out where the Sex begins
Don Herold
– a cage to catch our dreams
John Huston
– a locality where people without reputation try to live up to it
– a place where the stars employ doubles to do all their dangerous jobs for them, except marriage
Tom Jenk
– the only town where you can die of encouragement
Pauline Kael
– a place where there is no definition of your worth earlier than your last picture
Murray Kempton
– a cultural desert
Maurice Maeterlinck
– a town where inferior people have a way of making superior people feel inferior
Dan F Malone
– a trip through a sewer in a glass-bottomed boat
Wilson Mizner
– a place where they'll pay you a thousand dollars for a kiss and fifty cents for your soul
Marilyn Monroe
– Californication
James Montgomery
– a place where you spend more than you make, on things you don't need, to impress people you don't like
Ken Murray
– a dreary industrial town controlled by hoodlums of enormous wealth, the ethical sense of a pack of jackals, and taste so degraded that it befouled everything to touch it
S J Perelman
– an empty wastepaper basket
Ginger Rogers
– an extraordinary kind of temporary place
John Schlesinger
– a place where they know only one word of more than one syllable, and that is *fillum*
Louis Sherwin

– a place where the inmates are in charge of the asylum
Laurence Stallings
– loneliness beside the swimming pool
Liv Ullman
– a town where there are basically two types of exercise: jogging and helping a recently divorced friend move
Robert Wagner
– the biggest electric train any boy ever had
Orson Welles
– a place where they place you under contract instead of under observation
– a town that has to be seen to be disbelieved
Walter Winchell
– a combination of Heaven, Hell and a lunatic asylum
Albert Williams
– Disneyland staged by Dante. You imagine purgatory is like this except that the parking is not so good
Robin Williams
– a rotten gold-plated sewer of a town
James Woods
– an entertaining place where swimming pools are bought and wedding rings are rented
Edmund H Volkart
(see also *actor, actress, cinema, film*)

home – the place you can go when you're whipped
Muhammad Ali
– an invention on which no one has yet improved
Ann Douglas
– a place where, when you have to go there, they have to take you in
Robert Frost
– where you hang yourself
A O Goetz
– where you hang your head
Groucho Marx
– where the college student home for the holidays isn't
Laurence J Peter
– where your garbage is
David Porter
– a place you grow up wanting to leave, and grow old wanting to get back to
John Ed Pearce
– the girl's prison and the woman's workhouse
George Bernard Shaw
– a place where part of the family waits till the rest of the family brings the car back
Earl Wilson
(see also *modern home*)

homeowner – a person who is always on his way to a hardware store
Herbert V Prochnow Jr

home pregnancy test – a chance to panic sooner
Joyce Armor

home-sickness – to want something back that was never there
Renate Rubinstein
– the only disease that does not require rest
H de Vere Stacpoole
– contraction of the soul
Jim Vuylsteke

homework – work that kids leave at home
Jasmine Birtles

'homo' – the legitimate child of the 'suffragette'
Wyndham Lewis

homosexual – just somebody who doesn't believe in mixed marriages
Milton Berle
– a female soul in a male body
Mae West

homosexuality – God's way of insuring that the truly gifted aren't burdened with children
Sam Austin
(see also *lesbianism*)

honest psychiatrist – one who will admit how much some of his patients help him
O A Battista
(see also *psychiatrist*)

honest politician – a national calamity
Robert Anton Wilson
– one whose political actions are not dictated by a desire to increase his own income
Bertrand Russell
(see also *politician*)

honesty – to believe in your own lies
Fernand Auwera
– the best policy unless you are a crook
Winston Groom
– the excuse of cowards
Ephraïm Kishon

– the most important thing in life. Unless you really know how to fake it, you'll never make it
Bernard Rosenberg
– what is said to be the best policy, except in the advertising and insurance industries
Edmund H Volkart

honeymooning – a very overrated occupation
Noël Coward

Hong Kong – a place where you went broke saving money
Shirley MacLaine

Honolulu – a place that's got everything. Sand for the children, sun for the wife, sharks for the wife's mother
Ken Dodd

honour – a badge that you cannot pin on yourself
O A Battista

hope *v.* – to give the lie to the future
E M Cioran

hope *n.* – delicate suffering
Imamu Amiri Baraka
– the parent of faith
Cyrus A Bartol
– the last refuge of the hopeless
Georges Elgozy
– tomorrow's veneer over today's disappointment
Evan Esar
– the feeling you have that the feeling you have isn't permanent
Jean Kerr
– a very unruly emotion
Gloria Steinem

hors d'oeuvre – a ham sandwich cut into forty pieces
Jack Benny

horse – an animal dangerous at both ends and uncomfortable in the middle
Ian Fleming
– the most important part of a jockey
Jean Giraudoux

hospital – an institution that is dedicated to the cure of disease – and modesty
Gene Perret

hospital bed – a parked taxi with the meter running
Frank Scully

hotel – a place that keeps the manufacturers of 25-watt bulbs in business
Shelley Berman

house – a machine for living
Le Corbusier
– a machine for loving in
Craig McGregor

House of Lords – something like a glass of champagne that has stood for five days
Clement Attlee
– the British Outer Mongolia for retired politicians
Tony Benn
– a model of how to care for the elderly
Frank Field
– the only club in the world where the proprietor pays for the drinks
Michael Foot
– five hundred men, ordinary men, chosen accidentally from among the unemployed
David Lloyd George
– an ermine-lined dustbin, an upmarket geriatric home with a faint smell of urine
Austin Mitchell
– a good evidence of life after death
Donald Soper
– a perfect eventide home
Mary Stocks
– an illusion to which I have never been able to subscribe – responsibility without power, the prerogative of the eunuch throughout the ages
Tom Stoppard

housewife – *pl.* sleep-in maids
Neil Simon
– the Cinderella of the affluent state
Edith Summerskill
(see also *wife*)

hula – welcome waggin'
Frank Tyger

human being – *pl.* the only creatures on earth that allow their children to come back home
Bill Cosby

– *pl.* timid punctuation marks sprinkled among the incomprehensible sentences of life
Jean Giraudoux
– an ingenious assembly of portable plumbing
Christopher Morley
– a very complicated physical mechanism and nothing more
J J C Smart
(see also *man*)

human body – the only machine for which there are no spare parts
Herman M Biggs
– the best
picture of the human soul*L*
dwig Wittgenstein

human ego – the only thing that can keep growing without nourishment
Marshall Lumsden
(see also *big egos, egoist*)

human history – the sad result of each one looking out for himself
Julio Cortâzar
– a race between education and catastrophe
H G Wells
(see also *history, political history*)

humanity – just a work in progress
Tennessee Williams

humility – the virtue of a doormat at the foot of the stairs
Antoon Vloemans

humour – a very serious matter
Fernand Auwera
– defeated sadness
Godfried Bomans
– something that thrives between man's aspirations and his limitations
Victor Borge
– just another defense against the universe
Mel Brooks
– grit in the evolutionary process
Heywood Broun
– merely tragedy standing on its head with its pants torn
Irving S Cobb
– the politeness of despair
Jean Cocteau
– sorrow standing on its head

Ernest Claes
– an affirmation of dignity, a declaration of man's superiority to all that befalls him
Romain Gary
– a universal language
Joel Goodman
– something that you had better laugh at
Piet Grijs
– laughing at what you haven't got when you ought to have it
Langston Hughes
– a type of stimulation which tends to elicit the laughter reflex
Arthur Koestler
– the kindly contemplation of the incongruities of life, and the artistic expression thereof
Stephen Leacock
– reason gone mad
Groucho Marx
– the healthy way of feeling 'distance' between one's self and the problem, a way of standing off and looking at one's problems with perspective
Rollo May
– a hole that lets the sawdust out of a stuffed shirt
Jan McKeithen
– practically the only thing about which the English are utterly serious
Malcolm Muggeridge
– the ability to see three sides of one coin
Ned Rorem
– a reminder that no matter how high the throne one sits on, one sits on one's bottom
Taki
– emotional chaos remembered in tranquillity
James Thurber
– the sense of the Absurd which is despair refusing to take itself seriously
Arland Ussher
– the smile of someone who knows how little reason there is to laugh
Julien de Valckenaere
– the champagne of the tears
Antoon van der Plaetse
– the first of the gifts to perish in a foreign tongue
Virginia Woolf
(see also *sense of humour*)

humorist – someone who doesn't really know whether to smile or to weep at what is happening around him
Fernand Auwera
– a man who feels bad but who feels good about it
Don Herold

– a fellow who realizes, first, that he is no better than anybody else, and second, that nobody else is either
Homer McLin

hunch – creativity trying to tell you something
Frank Capra

hunger – the hunting-dog of death
W F Hermans

hunter – a killer who has found a way to satisfy his instincts legally
Alain Germoz

husband – one who stands by his wife in troubles she'd never had if she hadn't married him
Jasmine Birtles
– the critic on the hearth
John S Crosbie
– the only thing that keeps a woman from being happily married
Andra Douglas
– a guy who tells you when you've got on too much lipstick and helps you with your girdle when your hips stick
Ogden Nash
– what is left of the lover after the nerve has been extracted
Helen Rowland
(see also *caring husband, ideal husband, married man*)

hustler – a man who will talk you into giving him a free ride and make it seem as if he is doing you a great favor
Bill Veeck

hypochondriac – someone who remembers how many measles he had
Colin Bowles
– one who has a pill for everything except what ails him
Mignon McLaughlin

hypocrisy – the lubricant of society
David Hull
– the Vaseline of social intercourse
J R Newman
– the most difficult and nerve-racking vice that any man can pursue; it needs an unceasing vigilance and a rare detachment of spirit. It cannot, like adultery or gluttony, be practised at spare moments; it is a whole-time job
W Somerset Maugham

hypocrite – a person who – but who isn't?
Don Marquis

i

i – the little finger of the alphabet
Ramón Gómez de la Serna

ice hockey – a form of disorderly conduct in which the score is kept
Doug Larson
(see also *hockey*)

icicle – a stiff piece of water
Fred Allen

idea – a feat of association
Robert Frost
– salvation by imagination
Frank Lloyd Wright
– putting truth in checkmate
José Ortega Y Gasset
– *pl.* information taking shape
Jim Rohn

ideal – a wall with nothing behind it
Adrien Vély

ideal government – despotism tempered by assassination
John C W Reith
(see also *government*)

ideal husband – the guy next door
Joey Adams
– one who treats his wife with the same consideration he treats his pretty secretary
O A Battista
(see also *caring husband, husband, married man*)

idealism – the noble toga that political gentlemen drape over their will to power
Aldous Huxley

idealist – one who helps the other fellow to make a profit
Henry Ford
– one who, on noticing that a rose smells better than a cabbage, concludes that it will also make better soup

H L Mencken
– a man with both feet planted firmly in the air
Franklin D Roosevelt
– someone who isn't going to achieve something
Arthur Scargill

ideal love – love that does not make you obliged to anything
Stef Bos
(see also *art of love, eternal love, fall in love, first love, love, platonic love, true love*)

ideal wife – a woman who knows all the favorite dishes of her husband – *and* the restaurants where you can eat them
Laura Antonelli
– one who remains faithful to you but tries to be just as charming as if she weren't
Sacha Guitry
– the one who left you
Olivier de Kersauson
– any woman who has an ideal husband
Booth Tarkington
(see also *modern wife, perfect wife, wife*)

ideal world – Disneyland without entrance fees
Mike Barfield
(see also *world*)

identity – a kind of negotiation individuals make with other individuals to give each other the illusion of separate independence
Chandler Brossard
– the crisis which you can't see
Marion Elliott
– what you can say you are according to what they say you can be
Jill Johnston
– the state of being of a person, which seems to be lost, since so many people are searching for one
Edmund H Volkart

if – a two letter word for 'futility'
Louis Phillips

ignorance – when you don't know something and somebody finds it out
Jethro Burns
– a voluntary misfortune
Nicholas Ling

ignorant person – is one who doesn't know what you have just found out
Will Rogers

illusions – the only certainties we have
Hans Warren

image – what colonizes the mind
John Henrik Clarke

imagination – the highest kite one can fly
Lauren Bacall
– the strongest nation on earth
– a poor substitute for experience
Havelock Ellis
– the memory of the future
Robert Sabatier
– intelligence having fun
George Scialabba

imitation – the sincerest form of television
Fred Allen

immigration – the sincerest form of flattery
Denis Norden
(also attributed to *Jack Paar*)

immobile – mobile phone after receipt of first call-bill
Mike Barfield
– state of motionless, the safest state of an automobile
Edmund H Volkart

immorality – the morality of those who are having a better time
H L Mencken

immortality – an overrated commodity
Samuel N Behrman
– a fate worse than death
Edgar A Shoaff
– the only cause you can't die for
Heathcote Williams

impeccable – unable to be eaten by a chicken
Ray Hand

implementation – the sincerest form of flattery
L Peter Deutsch

impotence – the difference between excess and ex-sex
Fernand Auwera
– the only quality of a man that is not hereditary
Georges Elgozy

impresario – a promoter with a cape
L L Levinson

impropriety – the soul of wit
W Somerset Maugham

incentive – the possibility of getting more money than you can earn
L L Levinson

incest – what must be kept in the family
Johan Anthierens
– relations with one's relations
Leonard Rossiter

incident – annoying word which your mother-in-law uses in reference to your wedding
Cy DeBoer

incinerator – a writer's best friend
Thornton Wilder

income tax – the only expense nowadays you can't charge to your credit card
Joey Adams
– the hardest thing in the world to understand
Albert Einstein
(see also *fair tax structure, taxes, wealth tax*)

income tax assessor – a person who follows you into a revolving door but comes out ahead of you
Colin Bowles

income tax returns – the most imaginative fiction being written today
Herman Wouk

indecision – the thief of opportunity
Jim Rohn

independent – the guy who wants to take the politics out of politics
Adlai Stevenson

indigestion – the difference between reality and romance
Faith Hines

individual – a multitude of one million divided by one million
Arthur Koestler

indolence – a word that makes my laziness seem classy
Bert Williams

industrial action – the continuation of negotiations by other means
Denis McShane

inebriate – a man who thinks the whole world revolves around him
O A Battista

inexperience – what makes a young man do what an older man says is impossible
Herbert V Prochnow

infant prodigy – a small child with highly imaginative parents
R H Creese

infinity – nature's way of putting things off
Don Addis
– the quickest shortcut to the unknown
Alan Harris
– time on an ego trip
Jane Wagner

inflation – one form of taxation that can be imposed without legislation
Milton Friedman
– prosperity with high blood pressure
Arnold H Glasgow

inflexibility – the hallmark of the Tiny Mind
John Sanborn

information – the currency of democracy
Ralph Nader

information highway – where the telephone, television and computer merge onto a single high-tech turnpike, with tollbooths stationed at regular intervals
Rick Bayan

in-laws – Trojan Horses
Theo Mestrum

insanity – a perfectly rational adjustment to the insane world
R D Laing
– building major structures upon foundations which do not exist
Norman Mailer

insect repellent – one of a number of joke items available in any chemist shop
Henry Beard

insider trading – stealing too fast
Calvin Trillin

insomnia – the result of worry over sleeping-pill side effects
Mike Barfield

inspiration – the moment when fact and fiction meet
Gys Miedema

insult – uncontrollable boomerang
Jan Deloof

insurance – a cross between betting and philosophy
Paul Jennings
– what you pay now so when you're dead you'll have nothing to worry about
Joseph Rosenbloom
– *pl.* trade in fear
Lévi Weemoedt
(see also *auto insurance, life insurance*)

insurance policy – something like old underwear. The gaps in its cover are only shown by accident
David Yates

integrity – to look as stupid as you really are
Toon Verhoeven

intellect – a poor instrument for discovering what goes on in the heart
Henry Root

intellectual – a man who doesn't know how to park a bike
Spiro Agnew
– someone who thinks a lot and earns a little
Marco A Almazàn
– *pl.* people who believe that ideas are of more importance than values. That is to say, their own ideas and other people's values
Gerald Brenan

– someone whose mind watches itself
Albert Camus
– an unsuccessful idiot
Frédéric Dard
– *pl.* the most intolerant of all people
Paul Durcan
– a man who takes more words than necessary to tell more than he knows
Dwight D Eisenhower
– someone who likes to explain to people the things he didn't understand either
André Frossard
– someone who knew Toulouse Lautrec before he saw the movie *Moulin Rouge*
Sacha Guitry
– a person whose intellect improves much faster than his income
Edmund H Volkart
– someone who has found something more interesting than sex
Edgar Wallace
– anybody who reads a morning newspaper
Arna-Maria Winchester

intellectual snob – someone who can listen to the William Tell Overture and not think of The Lone Ranger
Dan Rather
(see also *snobs*)

intelligence – that faculty of mind, by which order is perceived in a situation previously considered disordered
Haneef A Fatmi
– perhaps only an instinct that is mistaken
Eugène Ionesco
– the body of the mind
Cor de Jonge
– quickness in seeing things as they are
George Santayana
(see also *artificial intelligence*)

intelligent woman – a woman with whom we can be as stupid as we like
Paul Valéry

see also *woman*)

intercourse – the pure, sterile, formal expression of men's contempt for women
Andrea Dworkin

Internal Revenue Service – the world's most successful mail-order business
Henny Youngman
(see also *IRS*)

Internet – something so big, so powerful and so pointless that for some people it is a complete substitute for life
Andrew Brown
the most intellectually stimulating waste of time you can find
Jeff Goslin
– the biggest net in the world; many have already been caught in it
Leo de Haes
– something like a herd of performing elephants with diarrhoea – massive, difficult to redirect, awe-inspiring, entertaining and a source of mind-boggling amounts of excrement when you least expect it
Gene Spafford

interpreter – someone who lies in two languages
Piet Grijs

interpretation – the revenge of the intellectual upon art
Susan Sontag

interview – an intimate conversation between journalist and politician wherein the journalist seeks to take advantage of the garrulity of the politician and the politician of the credulity of the journalist
Emery Kelen

intuition – a suspension of logic due to impatience
Rita Mae Brown
– the alibi for the poor of mind
Jan Greshoff
– reason in a hurry
Holbrook Jackson
– the least unreliable certainty
Fernand Lambrecht

inventing – a combination of brains and materials. The more brains you use, the less materials you need
Charles F Kettering

invention – the mother of necessity
Thorsten Veblen

investigating journalist – one who can think up plausible scandals
Lambert Jeffries
(see also *good journalist, journalist, rock journalism*)

Iranian moderate – one who has run out of ammunition
Henry Kissinger

Ireland – the old sow that eats her farrow
James Joyce
– a country full of genius, but with absolutely no talent
Hugh Leonard
– a collection of secret societies
V S Pritchett

Irish coffee – a drink providing in a single glass all four essential food groups: alcohol, caffeine, sugar and fat
Alex Levine
(see also *coffee, English coffee*)

Irishman – the only man in the world who will step over the bodies of a dozen naked women to get to a bottle of stout
Anon
– *pl.* street angels and house devils
Edna O'Brien
– a human enthymeme – all extremes and no middle
Austin O'Malley

Irish queer – a fellow who prefers women to drink
Sean O'Faolain

ironing – the perpetuum mobile of the household
Simon Carmiggelt

irony – hygiene of the mind
Elizabeth A Bibesco
– cousin of impotency
Wojciech Mlynarski
– a form of lucidity, it is a cooling off the mind
Anaïs Nin
– tenderness that feels ashamed
Etienne Rey

irritation – raising your children under the eyes of your parents
Jasmine Birtles

IRS – Infernal Revenue Service
Anon
(see also *Internal Revenue Service*)

Israel – the only country where one can say of someone that he is a Jew without being an anti-Semite
Jean-Paul Sartre

Italy – a poor country full of rich people
Richard Gardner

j

jade – a semiprecious stone or a semiprecious woman
Oliver Herford

jail – place where they keep the litter of the law
L L Levinson

jam – a commodity found on bread, children and door-handles
Jasmine Birtles

jazz – the sound of surprise
Witney Balliett
– the only form of art existing today in which there is freedom of the individual without the loss of group contact
Dave Brubeck
– music that is illiterate, instinctual, impulsive, aleatoric, unscorable, unpredictable – and that's its charm
Anthony Burgess
– the only music in which the same note can be played night after night but differently each time
Ornette Coleman
– American classic music
Willis Conover
– the result of the energy stored up in America
George Gershwin
– hot chocolate on frozen tears
Piet Grijs
– democracy in music
Wynton Marsalis
– a symbol of the triumph of the human spirit, not of its degradation. It is a lily in spite of the swamp
Archie Shepp

– music invented by devils for the torture of imbeciles
Henry van Dyke
– music that came to America 300 years ago in chains
Paul Whiteman
(see also *music*)

jazz musician – a juggler who uses harmonies instead of orangies
Benny Green

jealousy – a lack of respect for the loved one
Ivan Bounine
– no more than feeling alone against smiling enemies
Elizabeth Bowen
– the vice of possession
Jacques Chardonne
– dragon which slays love under the pretence of keeping it alive
Havelock Ellis
– invariably a symptom of neurotic insecurity
Robert Heinlein
– all the fun you think they had
Erica Jong
– the poison in female friendships
Monika Sauwer
– the tribute mediocrity pays to genius
Fulton Sheen
– a lack of confidence, especially self-confidence
Eric van der Steen
– the thermometer of love
Herwig Verleyen

Jehova – a God with many witnesses but never an alibi
Piet Grijs

Jehova's Witnesses – people with very strong feet
Mark Uytterhoeven

jewelry – a woman's best friend
Edna Ferber

Jewish novel – a story in which boy meets girl, boy gets girl and then worries what his mother will say
Colin Bowles
(see also *novel*)

Jewish nymphomaniac – a woman who will make love with a man

the same day she has her hair done
Maureen Lipman
(see also *nymphomaniac*)

job – death without the dignity
Brendan Behan

jogger – a pedestrian who's going down a dark street
Milton Berle

jogging – something for people who aren't intelligent enough to watch breakfast television
Victoria Wood

John Paul II – one of the few Polish guys who could find a job in Italy
José Artur

joke – a kind of *coitus interruptus* between reason and emotion
Arthur Koestler

journalism – that with which you may fill the space between advertisements
Imre Békessy
– the only thinkable alternative to working
Jeffrey Bernard
– the only job that requires no degrees, no diplomas, and no specialised knowledge of any kind
Patrick Campbell
– a sure way of using up your intellectual capital
John Maddox
– the second oldest profession
Robert Sylvester
– the ability to meet the challenge of filling space
Rebecca West

journalist – the historian of his time
Oriana Fallaci
– an author that is certain of being published
Sigmund Graff
(see also *good journalist, investigating journalist, rock journalism*)

joy – the feeling of grinning inside
Melba Colgrove
– a fruit that Americans eat green
Amando Zegri

judge – a jurist who has to decide which party had the best lawyer
Fons Jansen
– a law student who marks his own papers
H L Mencken

junk – anything that has outlived its usefulness
Oliver Herford

jury – twelve persons who are to decide which party has the better lawyer
Robert Frost

justice – unjustice reasonably divided
Maurice Chapelan
– the sanction of established injustice
Anatole France
– the longest distance between two points
Georges Guilbert
– a decision in your favor
Harry Kaufman

just peace – when our side gets what it wants
Bill Mauldin

juvenile delinquent – a teenager who wants what he wants when he wants it and won't wait to get it
C F Murphy

k

karate – a form of martial arts in which people who have had years and years of training can, using only their hands and feet, make some of the worst movies in the history of the world
Dave Barry

keyhole – a low-tech personal surveillance device
Mike Barfield

kids – the best form of contraception
Jasmine Birtles
– little stupid people who live in your house and don't pay rent
Rick Reynolds
(see also *child*)

killing – an excellent way of dealing with a hostility problem
Theodore J Flicker

– the ultimate simplification of life
Hugh MacDiarmid

killing time – the chief end of our society
Ugo Betti

kilt – an unrivalled garment for fornication and diarrhoea
John Masters

kiss – a lovely trick designed by nature to stop speech when words become superfluous
Ingrid Bergman
– nothing divided by two
Peter Darbo
– the anatomical juxtaposition of two *orbicularis oris* muscles in a state of contraction
Henry Gibbons
– to a young girl, faith; to a married woman, hope; to an old maid, charity
V P Skipper

kissing – a means of getting two people so close together that they can't see anything wrong with each other
René Yasenek

kitchenette – a narrow aisle that runs between a gas stove and a can of tomatoes
Bob Burns

kitsch – the echo of art
Kurt Tucholsky

kleptomaniac – a person who helps himself because he can't help himself
Henry Morgan

knowledge – knowing as little as possible
Charles Bukowski
– the only instrument of production that is not subject to diminishing returns
J M Clark
– a deadly friend when no one sets the rules.
The fate of all mankind, I see, is in the hands of fools.
King Crimson
– power, if you know it about the right person
Ethel Watts Mumford

l

ladle – the only thing that is edible in a pot of leek soup
Henry Beard

lady – a woman who can hold a man in her grip without ever letting him come within an arm's length of her
O A Battista
– one who never shows her underwear unintentionally
Lillian Day
– *pl.* people who do not do things themselves
Gwen Raverat
(see also *woman*

lambada – choreographed sex
Joe Baltake
(see also *ballet, chat-chat-chat, dance, tango*)

language – all that separates us from the lower animals, and the bureaucrats
Jerry Adler
– the first portable instrument invented by man
Vincenzo Agnetti
– an attempted murder of reality
Ingeborg Bachmann
– a virus from outer space
William S Burroughs
– a wonderful thing. It can be used to express thoughts, to conceal thoughts, but more often, to replace thinking
Kelly Fordyce
– air pollution
Piet Grijs
– the fatherland which we never can leave
Irina Grivnina
– the purest instrument of culture
Vàclav Havel
– a kind of human reason, which has its own internal logic of which man knows nothing
Claude Lévi-Strauss
– a form of organized stutter
Marshall McLuhan
– the source of all misunderstandings

Antoine de Saint-Exupéry
– the main instrument of man's refusal to accept the world as it is
George Steiner
– a dialect with an army and navy
Max Weinreich

laugh – a smile that burst
John E Donovan

laughter – an instant vacation
Milton Berle
– the closest distance between two people
Victor Borge
– the first evidence of freedom
Rosario Castellanos
– a form of internal jogging
Norman Cousins
– human expression of joy or pleasure, last heard in England in 1979
Tony Dunham
– a tranquilizer with no side effects
Arnold H Glasgow
– a safe and civilized alternative to violence
Martin Grotjahn
– an orgasm triggered by the intercourse of reason with unreason
Jack Kroll
– the most civilized music in the world
Peter Ustinov
– the brush that sweeps away the cobwebs of the heart
Mort Walker

lava – the earth burning its mouth
Hans-Horst Skupy

lavatory – volcano
Ray Hand
(see also *bathroom, flush toilet*)

lavatory seat – euphemism for an inner-city constituency
Mike Barfield

law – a business whose outlook is shared by its major clients
Laura Nader
– a reflection and a source of prejudice. It both enforces and suggests forms of bias
Diane B Schulder
– the backbone which keeps man erect
S C Yuter

lawyer – *pl.* the operators of the toll bridge which anyone in search of justice must pass
Jane Bryant Quinn
– one who protects us against robbers by taking away the temptation
H L Mencken

laziness – vice that protects you from many other vices
Paul Jacobs
– the mother of nine inventions out of ten
Philip K Saunders

leader – a man who has the ability to make other people do what they don't want to do, and like it
Harry S Truman

leadership – the only real training for leadership
Anthony Jay
– getting someone to do what they don't want to do in order to achieve what they want to achieve
Tom Landry
– the challenge to be something more than average
Jim Rohn
– the only safe ship in a storm
Faye Wattleton

leading authority – anyone who has guessed right more than once
Frank A Clark

learning – finding out what you already know
Richard Bach
– suddenly understanding something you've understood all your life, but in a new way
Doris Lessing

lease-car – dummy for managers
Pieter Klaas Jagersma

leaves – the verbs that conjugate the seasons
Gretel Ehrlich

lecture – an occasion when you numb one end to benefit the other
John Gould
– a process by which the notes of the professor become the notes of the students without passing through the minds of either
R K Rathbun

left – a group of people who will never be happy unless they can convince themselves that they are about to be betrayed by their leaders
Richard Crossman

legend (*person*) – the consecration of fame
Coco Chanel

legend (*story*) – a lie that has attained the dignity of age
H L Mencken
(see also *myth*)

leisure – the opiate of the masses
Malcolm Muggeridge

leopard – a form of dotted lion
L L Levinson

lesbianism – the greatest threat that exists to male supremacy
Rita Mae Brown
(see also *homosexuality*)

liar – one who tells an unpleasant truth
Oliver Herford

liberal – a man who cultivates the skills that make freedom operational
Max Ascoli
– a future conservative
Kazimierz Bartoszewic
– a man or a woman or a child who looks forward to a better day, a more tranquil night, and a bright, infinite future
Leonard Bernstein
– a man who leaves the room when the fight starts
Heywood Broun
– a man who will give away everything he doesn't own
Frank Dane
– *pl.* the flying saucers of politics. No one can make head nor tail of them and they never are twice seen in the same place
John G Diefenbaker
– a man too broadminded to take his own side in a quarrel
Robert Frost
– a man who tells other people what to do with their money
Leroi Jones
– a power worshipper without power
George Orwell
– a person whose interests aren't at stake at the moment
Willis Player

liberalism – the supreme form of generosity; it is the right which the majority concedes to minorities and hence it is the noblest cry that has ever resounded on this planet
José Ortega y Gasset
– the first refuge of political indifference and the last refuge of Leftists
Harry Roskolenko

liberated woman – one who has sex before marriage and a job after
Gloria Steinem
(see also *woman*)

liberty – a different kind of pain from prison
T S Eliot
– the right to tell people what they do not want to hear
George Orwell
– the ability to choose
Simone Weil
– the only thing you cannot have unless you are willing to give it to others
William Allen White

library – room where the murders take place
J B Morton
– thought in cold storage
Herbert Samuel

liquorice – the liver of candy
Michael O'Donoghue

lie – the wilful invention of facts that do not exist
Fidel Castro
– the basic building block of good manners
Quentin Crisp
– the truth, dressed and not bare
Peter Darbo
– that which you do not believe
Holbrook Jackson
– something that hadn't happened but might just as well have
Judith Rossner
– the ultimate proof of a lack of love
Julien Schoenaerts
– an abomination unto the Lord and a very pleasant help in time of trouble
Adlai Stevenson
– a child of the truth, begotten by fantasy
Wim Triesthof

life – Olympic Games, sponsored by a bunch of idiots
Ryùnosuke Akutagawa
– a concentration camp. You're stuck here, and there's no way out, and you can only rage impotently against your persecutors
Woody Allen
– a traveller who lets his suitcase drag behind him to cover his tracks
Louis Aragon
– the permission to know death
Djuna Barnes
– a long lesson in humility
James M Barrie
– a one-way-street with a dead end
O A Battista
– a box of sardines and we are all looking for the key
Alan Bennett
– 10 per cent what you make it and 90 per cent how you take it
Irving Berlin
– a partial, continuous, progressive, multiform and conditionally interactive self-realization of the potentialities of atomic electron states
J D Bernal
– a process of filling in time until the arrival of death or Santa Claus
Eric Berne
– a practical joke
Paul Bocuse
– a battle between Bad and Worse
Joseph Brodsky
– a dance party for cripples
Herman Brusselmans
– turning around between beds and coffins
Italo Calvino
– a moderately good play with a badly written third act
Truman Capote
– a tragedy when seen in close-up, but a comedy in long-shot
Charlie Chaplin
– a horizontal fall
Jean Cocteau
– just an elaborate metaphor for cricket
Marvin Cohen
– a maze in which we take the wrong turning before we have learnt to walk
Cyril Connolly
– a funny thing that happened to me on the way to the grave
Quentin Crisp
– just a bowl of pits
Rodney Dangerfield
– a zoo in a jungle
Peter De Vries

– death's vacation
J A Emmens
– a meaningless comma in the sentence of time
Chris Garratt & Mick Kidd
– finding different taskmasters
Marvin Gaye
– the only sentence which doesn't end with a period
Lois Gould
– a do-it-yourself project
Bill Greene
– a steady walk with a hidden precipice at the end
Lambert Jeffries
– a concatenation of ephemeralities
Alfred Kahn
– a tale told by an idiot, full of funny sounds and phooey
Hyman Kaplan
– a great big canvas, and you should throw all the paint on it you can
Danny Kaye
– an effort that deserves a better cause
Karl Kraus
– a sexually transmitted disease and the mortality rate is one hundred per cent
R D Laing
– is something to do when you can't get to sleep
Fran Lebowitz
– what happens while you are making other plans
John Lennon
– a tragedy full of joy
Bernard Malamud
– a party that you join after it's started and you leave before it's finished
Elsa Maxwell
– a mixed blessing, which we vainly try to unmix
Mignon McLaughlin
– a game of chance, in which we are the stakes
Gys Miedema
– one long postponement
Henry Miller
– only theatre, and mostly cheap melodrama at that
Malcolm Muggeridge
– the ever dwindling period between abortion and euthanasia
Patrick Murray
– a series of footnotes to a vast, obscure unfinished masterpiece
Vladimir Nabokov
– stepping down a step or sitting in a chair,
  And it isn't there.
Ogden Nash

– accepting what is and working from that
Gloria Naylor
– an offensive, directed against the repetitious mechanism of the Universe
Alfred North Whitehead
– a deadly disease
Louis Nucéra
– a series of movements from one chair to another
Austin O'Malley
– a solitary cell whose walls are mirrors
Eugene O'Neill
– a big party, but not everybody is invited
Manuel Puig
– a game whose rules each of us invents for himself
Alain Robbe-Grillet
– a series of crises separated by brief periods of self-delusion
Richard Rosen
– nothing but a competition to be the criminal rather than the victim
Bertrand Russell
– a shit sandwich and every day you take another bite
Joe Schmidt
– a series of inspired follies
George Bernard Shaw
– a man trying to get a partially inflated rubber lilo into a suitcase slightly too small to take it even when *un*inflated
N F Simpson
– a gamble at terrible odds, if it was a bet you wouldn't take it
Tom Stoppard
– the same damn thing over and over
Edna St. Vincent Millay
– a series of improbable situations with impossible people
Sidney Tremayne
– a lifelong death sentence
Julian Tuwim
– an overlong drama through which we sit being nagged by the vague memories of having read the reviews
John Updike
– a short, strange farce
Jos Vandeloo
– a present, but we have to pay for it
Eric van der Steen
– a whole series of circumstances beyond your control
Bruce W van Roy
– a fairy tale for grown-ups, told by children
Albrecht Vergheynst
– an unbroken succession of false situations
Thornton Wilder

– an accumulation of all the forces that resist death
Heathcote Williams
– unanswered question, but let's still believe in the dignity and importance of the question
Tennessee Williams
(see also *happy life*)

life insurance – death insurance
Russell Ash
– one of the least risky methods of pickpocketing
Jaap van de Merwe
(see also *auto insurance, insurance*)

light-year – a year that has 40 per cent less calories than a regular year
Milton Berle

limbo – place where arms and legs go when they die
Ray Hand

litigation – the basic legal right which guarantees every corporation its decade in court
David Porter

limited nuclear war – belief that a nuclear war in which not quite everyone is annihilated is possible
Russell Ash

lipstick – a device to make every kiss tell
L L Levinson

lisp – to call a spade a thspade
Oliver Herford

listening – the sincerest form of flattery
Joyce Brothers

literary agent – somebody whom you pay to make bad blood between yourself and your publisher
Angela Thirkell

literature – the question minus the answer
Roland Barthes
– the memory of humanity
Isaac Bashevis Singer
– the total dream of man
Graham Hough

– pure honey distilled from lies
Györgyi Konràd
– shame conquered by style
Gerrit Krol
– a sort of disciplined technique for arousing certain emotions
Iris Murdoch
– news that *stays* news
Ezra Pound
– proclaiming in front of everyone what one is careful to conceal from one's immediate circle
Jean Rostand
– an analysis of experience and a synthesis of the findings into a unity
Rebecca West
– the orchestration of platitudes
Thornton Wilder
(see also *great literature, today's literature)*

litter – a disgusting way of proving your affluence
Henry Bolte

live – a verb that only can be conjugated in the present tense
François Cavanna
– to postpone suicide day after day
Stig Dagerman
– the only known way to die
H Drion
– to pretend not to be dead
Jacques Dutronc
– to survive a dead child
Jean Genet
– a game of poker with death
Frank Herzen

living – the dead on holiday
Maurice Maeterlinck
(see also *art of living*)

llama – a woolly sort of fleecy hairy goat,
With an indolent expression and an undulating throat.
Hilaire Belloc

lobbyists – the touts of protected industries
Winston Churchill

locomotive – an insane reason to commit a crime
Johnny Hart

logic – any line of reasoning that confirms your conviction
O A Battista
– the art of going wrong with confidence
Joseph Wood Krutch

loitering – the crime of doing nothing in particular, particularly in public
Rick Bayan

London – a great cesspool into which all the loungers of the Empire are irresistibly drained
Arthur Conan Doyle
– a place you go to get bronchitis
Fran Lebowitz

loneliness – the wealth of the rich
Albert Camus
– the universal problem of rich people
Joan Collins
– to be alone with your blood
Freek de Jonge
– a constant companion to loving
Bettye J Parker-Smith
– a wall painted on a window
Bernard Seulsten
– the ultimate poverty
Abigail Van Buren
– poison of the weak, salt of the strong
Frans de Wilde

longevity – the revenge of talent upon genius
Cyril Connolly

long walk – the best remedy for a short temper
Jacqui Lee Schiff

Los Angeles – a city where the only cultural advantage is that you can make a right turn on a red light
Woody Allen
a city with all the personality of a paper cup
Raymond Chandler
– a watering hole for mad animals
Sammy Davis
– the plastic asshole of the world
William Faulkner
– seventy-two suburbs in search of a city
Dorothy Parker

loser – an innocent bystander who gets killed after a battle by an unexploded shell and then has his name spelled wrongly in the newspapers
Colin Bowles
– a stowaway on a kamikaze plane
Charlie Manna
(see also *good loser*)

lottery – undemocratic game: the majority never wins
Ugo Tognazzi

louse – a cow in the eyes of a microbe
Nico Scheepmaker

love *v.* – to escape through one being the mediocrity of others
Abel Bonnard
– to stop comparing
Bernard Grasset
– a transitive verb
Henry S Haskins
– to think of nothing else
Robert Sabatier
to look together in the same direction
Antoine de Saint-Exupéry
– not ever having to say you're sorry
Erich Segal
– to share selfishness with somebody else
Bernard Seulsten
– to receive a glimpse of heaven
Karen Sunde
– marrying rich and hoping she stays alive
Mark Uytterhoeven
(see also *art of love, fall in love*)

love *n.* – stuttering body-language
Ludwig Alene
– an underestimated form of schizophrenia
Marc Andries
– another problem that Karl Marx didn't solve
Jean Anouilh
– the victim's response to the rapist
Ti-Grace Atkinson
– the only bearable form of selfishness
Fernand Auwera
– just a system for getting someone to call you darling after sex
Julian Barnes

– an exploding cigar we willingly smoke
Lynda Barry
– the delightful interval between meeting a beautiful girl and discovering that she looks like a haddock
John Barrymore
– a game that is subject to the biggest penalties if not played fairly
O A Battista
– the only game in which two can play and both can lose
Texas Bix Bender
– an obsessive delusion that is cured by marriage
Karl Bowman
– one of the leading causes of life
Ashleigh Brilliant
– what makes the world go around – that and clichés
Michael Brooke Symons
– a narcissism shared by two
Rita Mae Brown
– hate without self-knowledge
Herman Brusselmans
– the greatest and most irresistible force in the world – and our hope of heaven
Barbara Cartland
– a poodle's chance of attaining the infinite
Louis-Ferdinand Céline
– the word used to label the sexual excitement of the young, the habituation of the middle-aged, and the mutual dependence of the old
John Ciardi
– to be vulnerable in the other
Mireille Cottenjé
– a burnt match skating in a urinal
Hart Crane
– the extra effort that we make in our dealings with those whom we do not like
Quentin Crisp
– the only effective counter to death
Maureen Duffy
– a passion entirely unrelated to our merits
Paul Eldridge
– desperate madness
John Ford
– a gamble, with our heart at stake
Fritz Francken
– the only sane and satisfactory answer to the problem of human existence
Erich Fromm
– a game that two can play and both win
Eva Gabor

– the effort a man makes to be satisfied with only one woman
Paul Géraldy
– the irresistible desire to be desired irresistibly
Louis Ginsberg
– an occupation for those who have no other
Antoine Gombaud
– a universal migraine,
A bright stain on the vision
Blotting out reason.
Robert Graves
the self-delusion we manufacture to justify the trouble we take to have sex
Dan Greenburg
– the drug which makes sexuality palatable in popular mythology
Germaine Greer
– the only game in which cheating forms part of the rules
Jan Greshoff
– a perky elf dancing a merry little jig and then suddenly he turns on you with a miniature machine gun
Matt Groening
– the key that unlocks the door of the visible to reveal a magnificent invisible
Alan Harris
– the only game that will never be postponed on account of rain
Homer Haynes
– an unselfish act that improves the quality of life of a living thing
Larry Hazen
– a hole in the heart
Ben Hecht
– that condition in which the happiness of another person is essential to your own
Robert A Heinlein
– something that hangs up behind the bathroom door and smells of Lysol
Ernest Hemingway
– a fanclub with only two fans
Adrian Henri
– a conflict between reflexes and reflections
Magnus Hirschfeld
– a wonderful thing and highly desirable in marriage
Rupert Hughes
– the most subtle form of self-interest
Holbrook Jackson
– the only fairy tale that ends with 'Once upon a time'
Hans Lohberger

– what we call the situation which occurs when two people who are sexually compatible discover that they can also tolerate one another in various other circumstances
Marc Maihueird
– to like his snoring more than an aria of Pavarotti
Amanda Marteleur
– temporary blindness for other beautiful women
Marcello Mastroianni
– the encounter of two weaknesses
François Mauriac
– the silent saying and saying of a single name
Mignon McLaughlin
– the delusion that one man or woman differs from another
H L Mencken
– a boogie-woogie of hormones
Henry Miller
– affection on the rocks
Michèle Morgan
– the extremely difficult realization that something other than oneself is real
Iris Murdoch
– an emotion experienced by the many and enjoyed by the few
George Jean Nathan
– a well that makes you thirsty
Marie Noël
– the cheapest of all religions
Cesare Pavese
– not the dying moan of a distant violin – it's the triumphant twang of a bedspring
S J Perelman
– sharing the problems you haven't got yet
Liselotte Pulver
– an attempt to change a piece of a dream-world into reality
Theodore Reik
– the common denominator
Alain Resnais
– the direct opposite of hate. By definition it's something you can't feel for more than a few minutes at a time, so what's all this bullshit about loving somebody for the rest of your life?
Judith Rossner
– what you feel for a dog or a pussycat. It doesn't apply to humans
– two minutes fifty-two seconds of squishing noises. It shows your mind isn't clicking right
Johnny Rotten
– woman's eternal spring and man's eternal fall
Helen Rowland

– a gross exaggeration of the difference between one person and everybody else
George Bernard Shaw
– the only disease that makes you feel better
Sam Shepard
– the best of opiates
Stevie Smith
– the dirty trick played on us to achieve continuation of the species
W Somerset Maugham
– a fruit in season at all times, and within reach of every hand
Mother Teresa
– the strange bewilderment which overtakes one person on account of another person
James Thurber
– to make of one's heart a swinging door
Howard Thurman
– a thirst that one cannot quench without becoming intoxicated
Sidney Tremayne
– the child of illusion and the parent of disillusion
Miguel de Unamuno
– an act of endless forgiveness, a tender look which becomes a habit
Peter Ustinov
– being stupid together
Paul Valéry
– more easily made than defined
Eric van der Steen
– listening to snoring without being annoyed
Renate van Gool
– the only reward we never earned
Jan Vercammen
– nothing but a giving, an exhaustless giving of one's very heart
Louis Wain
– a duel in which one of the two does not shoot
J W F Werumeus Buning
– another four-letter word
Tennessee Williams
– a feeling you feel when you're about to feel a feeling you never felt before
Flip Wilson
(see also *art of love, eternal love, fall in love, first love, ideal love, platonic love, romance, true love*)

love affairs – simply servings of self-pity for two
Alan Brien

love letters – the campaign promises of the heart
Robert Friedman

lover – someone who loves me instead of me
Fernand Auwera
– someone who gives as much consideration to your warts as you do, and continues to admire you as you do
Alan Brien
(see also *perfect lover*)

love song – a caress set to music
Sigmund Romberg

luck – what you have left after you give one hundred per cent
Langston Coleman
– when your burst of energy doesn't run afoul of someone else's
Mignon McLaughlin
– the residue of design
Branch Rickey
– a matter of preparation meeting opportunity
Oprah Winfrey
(see also *good luck*)

lunatic asylum – the place where optimism most flourishes
Havelock Ellis

lunch – the scientific name for an animal that doesn't either run from or fight its enemies
Michael Friedman

lusting – what keeps a lot of men going into old age
Dustin Hoffman

luxury – being alone in the bathroom
Cy DeBoer
– the art of idiots
Henri Duvernois

luxury dinner – a bad play surrounded by water
Clive James

lying – an indispensable part of making life tolerable
Bergen Evans
– a leech that has sucked truth dry
Max Frisch
– an elementary means of self-defence
Susan Sontag

lynching – the aftermath of slavery
Mary Church Terrell

m

macadam – first man born in Scotland
Bill McGarden

mad – a term we use to describe a man who is obsessed with one idea and nothing else
Ugo Betti

Madison Avenue – the Dream Street of hucksters where consumers are lulled to sleep
Edmund H Volkart

mad money – a psychiatrist's fee
Larry Wilde
(see also *money*)

madness – nobility of soul
At odds with circumstance.
Theodore Roethke

magnate – magnet for gold
Carlos de Vriese

magnum opus – a book which when dropped from a three-storey building is big enough to kill a man
Edward Wilson

major writing – to say what has been seen, so that it need never be said again
Delmore Schwartz
(see also *art of writing, writing*)

make-up – the veil of the Western woman
Nawal El Saadawi

making love – the sovereign remedy for anguish
Frédérick Leboyer
(see also *coitus, sex*)

male – a domestic animal which, if treated with firmness and kindness, can be trained to do most things
Jilly Cooper

– *pl.* a vast breeding experiment run by females
Irven De Vore
(see also *man, modern man, real man*)

male chauvinism – a shrewd method of extracting the maximum work for the minimum of compensation
Michael Korda

male menopause – the time when a man starts turning off the lights for economical rather than romantic reasons
John Merino

mallennium – a thousand years of shopping
Troy Dickson

man (*the male*) – just a woman's strategy for making other women
Margaret Atwood
– the second strongest sex in the world
Philip Barry
– the useless piece of flesh at the end of a penis
Jo Brand
– the only creature who refuses to be what he is
Albert Camus
– the only animal that plays poker
Don Herold
– an intelligence in servitude to his organs
Aldous Huxley
– *pl.* the funniest things since silly putty
Florence King
– creature with two legs and eight hands
Jayne Mansfield
– a creature who runs out of money even faster than he runs out of love
Mignon McLaughlin
– *pl.* nicotine-soaked, beer-besmeared, whisky-greased, red-eyed devils
Carry Nation
– one who loses his illusions first, his teeth second, and his follies last
Helen Rowland
– the missing link between the ape and the human being
Vicky Satter
– a failed boy
John Updike
(see also *male, man, modern man, real man*)

man (*the human being*) – an animal that plays Bach with his paws
Bertus Aafjes
– a history-making creature who can neither repeat his past nor leave it behind
W H Auden
– a riddle, not worth being resolved
Yvan Audouard
– a minutely set, ingenious machine for turning, with infinite artfulness, the red wine of Shiraz into urine
Karen Blixen
– the sum of all the social conditions of all times
Bertolt Brecht
– a puny, slow, awkward, unarmed animal
Jacob Bronowski
– the only creature that is his own parody
C Buddingh'
– a monkey that went in the wrong direction
François Cavanna
– an animal that thinks he can think
Jan G Elburg
– the only animal for whom his own existence is a problem which he has to solve
Erich Fromm
– a handshake between spirit and matter
Alan Harris
– a corpse poisoned with life
W F Hermans
– a dog's idea of what God should be
– the only animal that can be a fool
Holbrook Jackson
– persona non grata
Stanislaw Jerzy Lec
– still the most extraordinary computer of all
John F Kennedy
– the only animal that learns by being hypocritical. He pretends to be polite and then, eventually, he *becomes* polite
Jean Kerr
– a monkey escaped from censorship
Gabriel Laub
– the only animal in the world to fear
D H Lawrence
– is the sum of his actions, of what he has done, of what he can do, nothing else
– a miserable pile of secrets
André Malraux

– the only eyewitness of the universe
Maurits Mok
– a butterfly that changes into a caterpillar
Henry de Montherlant
– a fact that speaks
Harry Mulisch
– the bad child of the universe
James Oppenheim
– the only creature that consumes without producing
George Orwell
– an imitation of something, and a very bad imitation
P D Ouspensky
– the only animal that improves by wearing clothes
Cesare Pavese
– the king of domestic animals
Sybren Polet
– a useless passion
Jean-Paul Sartre
– a clever animal who behaves like an imbecile
Albert Schweitzer
– a more or less intelligent fool
Sim
– a complex being: he makes deserts bloom and lakes die
Gil Stern
– a creature that in the long run has got to believe in order to know, and to know in order to do
Allen Tate
– the best computer we can put aboard a spacecraft . . . and the only one that can be mass produced with unskilled labour
Wernher von Braun
– a hating rather than a loving animal
Rebecca West
(see also *human being, modern man*)

management – always trying to fine-tune the solution before it defines the problem
Wayne Aman
– the art of getting other people to do all the work
Maxim Drabon
– an organization that makes it difficult for other people to work
– the substitution of thought for brawn and muscle, of knowledge for folklore and superstition, and of co-operation for force
Peter F Drucker
– an activity or art where those who have not yet succeeded and those who have proved unsuccessful are led by those who have not yet failed
Paulsson Frenckner

manager – an artist who has inspiration worked out by others
Gys Miedema

managing – getting paid for home runs someone else hits
Casey Stengel

man-hating – a refusal to suppress the evidence of one's experience with men
Cheris Kramarae & Paula A Treichler

manipulation – violence with gloves on
Fernand Auwera
– persuading people to make up their minds while withholding some of the facts from them
Harold Evans

manners – the noise you don't make eating soup
L L Levinson
– the lowest common denominator of ethical experience
Victor S Navasky

man of manners – one who gets out of the bath to fart
Jasmine Birtles

manuscript – something submitted in haste and returned at leisure
Oliver Herford

marijuana – nature's way of saying 'high'
Peter Darbo

market – a huge whole in which you can lose your profits
Janwillem van de Wetering

marketing – the process of anticipating, specifying and satisfying the future needs of customers
David Coats
– sales with a college education
John Freund

market research – what you call it when you already know the answer you want, but still hunt up the question that will produce it
Robert Fuoss

marriage – the only union that cannot be organized. Both sides think they are management
William J Abley

marriage

– that relation between man and woman in which the independence is equal, the dependence mutual, and the obligation reciprocal
Louis K Anspacher
– an insurance-policy you sign without reading the small print
Fernand Auwera
– the quickest way to ruin a relationship
Shirley Bassey
– an indissoluble contract in which one party obtains from the other party more than either ever may hope to repay
O A Battista
– a knot tied by a minister and untied by a lawyer
Milton Berle
– the last subject to be effectively computerised
Drusilla Beyfus
– the most advanced form of warfare in the modern world
Malcolm Bradbury
– an arrangement by which two people start by getting the best out of each other and often end by getting the worst
Gerald Brenan
– the only lifelong conviction from which to escape with bad behaviour
Henry Brun
– the cause of adultery
Léo Campion
– a dangerous accident, which you will survive
René Clair
– a wonderful invention, but then again so is a bicycle repair kit
Billy Connolly
– an ideal situation for women who like to do nothing
Mireille Cottenjé
– the tomb of a wild romance
Benedetto Croce
– a woman too much and a man too little
Francis de Croisset
– a form of legalized rape.
Billy Crystal
– a necessary preliminary step towards being divorced
Justice Darling
– a life insurance for lazy women
Renate Dorrestein
– not a word but a sentence
Maxim Drabon
– two people agreeing to tell the same lie
Karen Durbin
– compared with going to bed with each other, this is a child's game
J A Emmens

– when a woman asks a man to remove his pyjamas because she wants to send them to the laundry
Albert Finney
– the aim and end of all sensible girls, because it is the meaning of life
Elinor Glyn
– a deal in which a man gives away half his groceries in order to get the other half cooked
John Gwynne
– the tragic beginning of a happy ending
Havank
– a ghastly public confession of a strictly private intention
Ian Hay
– the conventional ending of a love affair
Oliver Herford
– an honorable agreement among men as to their conduct toward women, and it was devised by women
Don Herold
– a mistake every man should make
George Jessel
– one huge afterplay
Freek de Jonge
– three-meals-a-day and remembering to carry out the trash
Joyce Brothers
– something like buying something you've been admiring for a long time in a shop window. You may love it when you get it home, but it doesn't always go with everything in the house
Jean Kerr
– a triumph of habit over hate
Oscar Levant
– a dramatic meeting between nature and civilization
Claude Lévi-Strauss
– a perfect moment frozen in a dull eternity
William Manville
– the refuge of the very lonely, and the very self-sufficient
Mignon McLaughlin
– three parts love and seven parts forgiveness of sins
Langdon Mitchell
– a vulgar effort on the part of dull people to bring boredom to a fine art
J B Morton
– adultery with your legal wife
Harry Mulisch
– the alliance of two people, one of whom never remembers birthdays and the other never forgets them
– the only known example of the happy meeting of the immovable object and the irresistible force
Ogden Nash

marriage

– a book of which the first chapter is written in poetry and the remaining chapters in prose
Beverley Nichols
– the meal where the soup is better than the dessert
Austin O'Malley
– something like paying an endless visit in your worst clothes
J B Priestley
– a lottery in which men stake their liberty and women their happiness
Virginie des Rieux
– an institution that simplifies life and complicates living
Jean Rostand
– a bargain, and somebody has to get the worst end of the bargain
Helen Rowland
– the only acceptable route to stemware
Paul Rudnick
– a love poem, but in prose
Robert Sabatier
– the best cure for love
Manuela Sarnitz-Miebach
– a stop on request
Clem Schouwenaars
– the unconditional surrender of the victor
Vittorio de Sica
– a sane form securing one from insane sex impulses and their consequences
Jean Toomer
– part of a sort of 50s revival package that's back in vogue along with neckties and naked ambition
Calvin Trillin
– the waste-paper basket of the emotions
Sidney James Webb
– a woman's best investment, because she can con some man into supporting her for the rest of his life
Alan Donald Whicker
– a bribe to make the housekeeper think she's a householder
Thornton Wilder
– a process of mummifying the corpse
P G Wodehouse
– a nonstop conversation
Betty Jane Wylie
– love gone – woman stays
Robert Zend
(see also *good marriage, happy marriage, wedding*)

married man – a single man with the nerve extracted
Jasmine Birtles
(see also *caring husband, husband, ideal husband, unmarried man*)

martyrdom – the only way in which a man can become famous without ability
George Bernard Shaw

Marxists – people whose insides are torn up day after day because they want to rule the world and no one will even publish their letter to the editor
Mark Helprin

mashed figs – a foodstuff that only your grandmother would eat, and only then because she couldn't find her dentures
Bill Bryson

masochist – a sadist, without opportunities
Cor Gilhuis

mass – everybody but me
Kadé Bruin
– the plural of no one
F J Schmit

mass murderers – people who have had *enough*
Quentin Crisp

master key – nightmare for crusaders
Guy Commerman

masterpiece – the latest opus by a commercially successful author or film-maker, esp. as proclaimed by shrewd reviewers who like to see themselves quoted in national ad campaigns
Rick Bayan

masturbation – sex with someone you love
Woody Allen
– shaking hands with the unemployed
George Carlin
– the thinking man's television
Christopher Hampton
– the primary sexual activity of mankind. In the nineteenth century, it was a disease; in the twentieth it's a cure
Thomas Szasz

mathematician – a device for turning coffee into theorems
Paul Erdos

mathematics – the only science where one never knows what one is talking about nor whether what is said is true
Bertrand Russell

matrimony – the root of all evil
Addison Mizner
– a process by which a grocer acquires an account the florist had
Francis Rodman

matter – a convenient formula for describing what happens where it isn't
Bertrand Russell

maturity – behaviour determined by the plans other people have in mind
David Mercer
– a high price for growing up
Tom Stoppard
– a bitter disappointment for which no remedy exists, unless laughter can be said to remedy anything
Kurt Vonnegut

MBA – acronym for several different but related terms: (1) Master of Business Administration; (2) Master Bull Artist; (3) Master of Blind Ambition
Robert Barron & Jim Fisk

meat – a status dish in which the sizzle counts for more than the intrinsic nutritional worth
Magnus Pyke

mechanic – a person who picks your pocket from underneath your car
Colin Bowles

media – just a word that has come to mean bad journalism
Graham Greene
– plural for mediocre
René Sasuisag
– sounds like a convention of spiritualists
Tom Stoppard

medicine – the one place where all the show is stripped of the human drama
Martin H Fischer

– a noble profession but a damn bad business
Humphrey Rolleston

meek – the people who will inherit the earth after the real estate has been sufficiently ravaged by the strong
Edmund H Volkart

meeting – an addictive, highly self-indulgent activity that corporations and other organizations habitually engage in only because they cannot actually masturbate
Dave Barry
– an event where minutes are taken and hours wasted
James C Kirk

megabyte – a nine-course dinner
Anon

megalomania – childhood disease of the dwarfs
Stanislaw Jerzy Lec

melancholy – the aftershave of sorrow
Johan Anthierens
– the hopeful idea that weeping is good for something
Piet Grijs
– amateur sadness
Jan Vercammen

memory – *pl.* hunting horns whose sound dies on the wind
Guillaume Apollinaire
– what is left when something happens and does not completely unhappen
Edward de Bono
– the other side of hope
Maurice Chapelan
– the thing you forget with
Alexander Chase
– the only paradise out of which we cannot be driven away
Sacha Guitry
– what the heart still knows after the brain has long forgotten it
Fernand Lambrecht
– a crazy woman that hoards coloured rags and throws away food
Austin O'Malley
– the painful inability to forget
Alexander Pola
– the wine cellar of the mind
Felix Timmermans
(see also *good memory*)

menus – the national dish of America
Robert Robinson

metaphor – the most fertile power possessed by man
José Ortega Y Gasset

metaphysics – almost always an attempt to prove the incredible by an appeal to the unintelligible
H L Mencken

Miami – a place where 1,000 different nationalities get together and give each other the finger
Richard Jeni

Miami beach – where neon goes to die
Lenny Bruce

microwave – oven invented just to prove that pub food *could* get worse
Mike Barfield
– signal from a friendly micro
Peter Darbo

middle age – when you are too young to take up golf and too old to rush up to the net
Franklin Pearce Adams
– a time of life
That man first notices in his wife.
Richard Armour
– having a choice of two temptations and choosing the one that will get you home earlier
Dan Bennett
– Youth Part II
Brickman
– a nice change from being young
Dorothy Canfield Fisher
– when a guy keeps turning off lights for economical rather than romantic reasons
Eli Cass
– when your old classmates are so grey and wrinkled and bald they don't recognize you
Bennett Cerf
– when you start to exchange your emotions for symptoms
Irving S Cobb
– the conflict between Mother Nature and Father Time
Peter Darbo

– when a narrow waist and a broad mind begin to change place
Glenn Dorenbush
– that time of life when a romantic dinner by candlelight seems less important than being able to read the menu clearly by lamplight
Sidney J Harris
– when your age starts to show around your middle
Bob Hope
– the time when a man is always thinking that in a week or two he will feel just as good as ever
Don Marquis
– half-way between your age and one hundred
R D Milligan
– anything over twenty and under ninety
A A Milne
– when you've met so many people that every new person you meet reminds you of someone else
– when you're sitting at home on Saturday night and the telephone rings and you hope it isn't for you
Ogden Nash
– when the best exercise is one of discretion
Laurence J Peter
– later than you think and sooner than you expect
Earl Wilson
(see also *age*)

middleness – the very enemy of the bold
Charles Krauthammer

militarism – one of the chief bulwarks of capitalism, and the day that militarism is undermined, capitalism will fail
Helen Keller

military intelligence – contradiction in terms
Oswald G Villard

mime – the art of speaking in silence
Gys Miedema

mind – a richly woven tapestry in which the colors are distilled from the experiences of the senses, and the design drawn from the convolutions of the intellect
Carson McCullers
– a strange machine which can combine the materials offered to it in the most astonishing ways
Bertrand Russell
– a woman's most erogenous zone
Raquel Welch

minister of finance – a legally authorised pickpocket
Paul Ramadier

minor surgery – what other people have
Bill Watson

miracle drug – any drug that will do what the label says it will do
Eric Hodgins
(see also *drug*)

miscellaneous – always the largest category
Joel Rosenberg

miser – a disagreeable contemporary, but an agreeable ancestor
Victor de Kowa

misery – a communicable disease
Martha Graham

misquotation – the pride and privilege of the learned
Hesketh Pearson

mistake – simply another way of doing things
Katharine Graham
– *pl.* the portals of discovery
James Joyce
– *pl.* part of the dues one pays for a full life
Sophia Loren
(see also *error*)

mistress – something that goes between a mister and a mattress
Joe E Lewis

mobile phone – the thin line between conspicuous success and standing in the street talking to yourself like a madman
Mike Barfield

modem – Monumentally Overpriced Data Eating Machine
Anon
– what landscapers do to dem lawns
Anon

moderation – a virtue only in those who are thought to have an alternative
Henry Kissinger

modern art – what happens when painters stop looking at girls and persuade themselves that they have a better idea
John Ciardi
(see also *art, abstract art, work of art*)

modern boss – one who would replace people with a computer, if he could find one that cringes
Milton Berle
(see also *boss*)

modern centaur – half a man and half a sportscar
Edith Grobleben

modern city – a place where you go out for a walk and get a breath of fresh air pollution
Joel Rothman
(see also *city*)

modern home – one where a switch can control everything but the children
Jasmine Birtles
(see also *home*)

modern man – any person born after Nietzsche's edict that 'God is dead' but before the hit recording 'I Wanna Hold Your Hand'
Woody Allen
(see also *male, man, real man*)

modern music – three farts and a raspberry, orchestrated
John Barbirolli
– the noise made by deluded speculators picking through the slagpile
Henry Pleasants
(see also *music*)

modern wife – a prostitute who doesn't deliver the goods
W Somerset Maugham
(see also *ideal wife, perfect wife, wife*)

modesty – the desire to be praised twice
Godfried Bomans
– ambition waiting for a better moment
C Buddingh'
– the hope that others will discover for themselves how great we really are
Aldo Cammarota
– a virtue that we must leave to others
Henri Duvernois

– a vastly overrated virtue
J K Galbraith
– an immodest word
J Goudsblom
– the gentle art of enhancing your charm by pretending not to be aware of it
Oliver Herford
– ashamed pride
Marcel Jouhandeau
– luxury only talented people can permit themselves
Fernand Lambrecht
– quality that contains its own objection
Harry Mulisch
– the opiate of the mediocre
Michael O'Hara
– the virtue of the half-hearted
Jean-Paul Sartre
(see also *false modesty*)

molehill – a mountain to the apprentice skier
Boris Evanoff

molehill man – a pseudo-busy executive who comes to work at 9 a.m. and finds a molehill on his desk. He has until 5 p.m. to make this molehill into a mountain. An accomplished molehill man will often have his mountain finished before lunch
Fred Allen

Monaco – the center of the spinning industry of the world
Oliver Herford

monarchy – the gold-filling in the mouth of decay
John Osborne
– a labour-intensive industry
Harold Wilson

monday – a depressing way to spend one-seventh of your life
Mary Kramer
– victim of Sunday
Jan Schepens

money – the manifestation of power
S E Anderson
– the only means to make you forget that you are not rich
Philippe Bouvard
– a more pleasant alternative to good advice
Colin Bowles

– what you'd get on beautifully without if only other people weren't so crazy about it
Margaret Case Harriman
– God in action
Frederick J Eikerenkoetter II
– just what we use to keep tally
Henry Ford
– just a few printed drawings to buy presents with
Johnny Halliday
– just something to make bookkeeping convenient
H L Hunt
– the most efficient labour-saving device
Franklin P Jones
– much more exciting than anything it buys
Mignon McLaughlin
– the poor people's credit card
Marshall McLuhan
– the only substance which can keep a cold world from nicknaming a citizen 'Hey, you!'
Wilson Mizner
– something good for bribing yourself through the inconveniences of life
Gottfried Reinhardt
– is power, freedom, a cushion, the root of all evil, the sum of blessings
Carl Sandburg
– a sixth sense without which you cannot make a complete use of the other five
W Somerset Maugham
– the most egalitarian force in society. It confers power on whoever holds it
Roger Starr
– the stuff with which one purchases time
Tom Stoppard
– the least viscous of all substances
Andrew Tron
– the mother's milk of politics
Jesse Unruh
(see also *mad money*)

monkey – a human being, retroactively
Piet Theys

monogamy – an obsolete word meaning a fidelity complex
J B Morton

monopoly – business at the end of its journey
Henry Demarest Lloyd

Marilyn Monroe – a vacuum with nipples
Otto Preminger

moon – nothing but a circumambulating aphrodisiac, divinely subsidized to provoke the world into a rising birth-rate
Christopher Fry

moonshiner – one who conducts his business in distill of the night
Dave Krieger

moose – an animal with horns on the front of his head, and a hunting lodge wall on the back of it
Groucho Marx

moral – what you feel good after
Ernest Hemingway

morale – self-esteem in action
Avery Weisman

moral indignation – in most cases 2 per cent moral, 48 per cent indignation and 50 per cent envy
Vittorio de Sica
– jealousy with a halo
H G Wells

morality – a private and costly luxury
Henry Brooks Adams
– contraband in war
Mahatma Gandhi
– a disease which progresses in three stages: virtue – boredom – syphilis
Karl Kraus
– what the majority then and there happen to like and immorality is what they dislike
Alfred North Whitehead
(see also *bourgeois morality*)

moral responsibility – what is lacking in a man when he demands it of a woman
Karl Kraus

morals – the taste for what is pure and what defies the era
Jacques Chardonne

more – the cry of the curious person
Bette Midler

Mormon – an American expatriate with four wives and one bicycle
Colin Bowles

morning sickness – breakfast television
Mike Barfield

mother – guilt-edged insecurity
Jasmine Birtles
– the child's supreme parent
Havelock Ellis
– the dead heart of the family, spending father's earnings on consumer goods to enhance the environment in which he eats, sleeps, and watches television
Germaine Greer

mother-in-law – the angel of divorce
Gaston Berger
– the backseat driver in the motorcar of child-rearing
Jasmine Birtles
– someone who goes too far when she gets too close
Alfredo La Mont

Mother Nature – a male chauvinist pig
Faith Hines

mothers – women who miscalculate
Abigail Van Buren

motivation – the art of getting people to do what you want them to do because they want to do it
Dwight D Eisenhower

mouth – outlet valve
Fritz Francken
– temporary refuge for lies
Piet Grijs

movie – a toupee made up to look like honest baldness
Pauline Kael
– *pl.* the only business where you can go out front and applaud yourself
Will Rogers

movie studio – the best toy a boy ever had
Orson Welles

MTV – the lava lamp of the 1980s
Doug Ferrari
(see also *television*)

mugwump – one of those boys who always has his mug on one side of the political fence and his wump on the other
Albert J Engel

multitasking – screwing up several things at once
Maxim Drabon

murder – an extroverted suicide
Graham Chapman

music – the best means we have of digesting time
W H Auden
– an art which can name the unnameable and communicate the unknowable
Leonard Bernstein
– the measure of mankind
Elias Canetti
– the refuge of souls ulcerated by happiness
E M Cioran
– the soul of geometry
Paul Claudel
– the augmentation of a split second of time
Erin Cleary
– a system of proportions in the service of a spiritual impulse
George Crumb
– just a means of creating a magical state
Robert Fripp
– the most expensive of all noises
Josef Hofmann
– the mother tongue of the heart
Ernst Hohenemser
– geometry in time
Arthur Honegger
– one of the ways God has of beating in on man
Charles Ives
– the human treatment of sounds
Jean-Michel Jarre
– the ability to be sad or happy without a reason
Tadeusz Kotarbinski

– a magic marriage between theology and the so diverting mathematic
Thomas Mann
– a beautiful opiate, if you don't take it too seriously
Henry Miller
– the way our memories sing to us across time
Lance Morrow
– mathematics you can hear
Harry Mulisch
– a medicine that's pleasant to take
Odetta
– another lady that talks charmingly and says nothing
Austin O'Malley
– the sole art which evokes nostalgia for the future
Ned Rorem
– a living application of mathematics
Gino Severini
– the brandy of the damned
George Bernard Shaw
– the outward and audible signification of inward and spiritual realities
Peter Warlock
– natural law as related to the sense of hearing
Anton von Webern
(see also *classical music, country music, good music, jazz musician, modern music, pop music, ragtime, rap, reggae music, rock and roll*)

musical – disorderly conduct occasionally interrupted by talk
George Ade
– *pl.* a series of catastrophes ending with a floor show
Oscar Levant
– *pl.* millions of pounds riding on a piece of piffle
Mark Steyn
(see also *Broadway musical*)

musical comedy – the Irish stew of drama. Anything may be put into it with the certainty that it will improve the general effect
P G Wodehouse
(see also *comedy, stand-up comedy*)

music critics – drooling, drivelling, doleful, depressing, dropsical drips
Thomas Beecham
(see also *critic, good critic, reviewmanship*)

musicologist – a man who can read music but cannot hear it
Thomas Beecham

music with dinner – an insult both to the cook and violinist
G K Chesterton

myth – *pl.* a way of solving the problem of making intelligible to the marketplace conclusions arrived at in the ivory tower
Adesanya Adebayo
– *pl.* gossip grown old
R P Blackmur
– a fixed way of looking at the world which cannot be destroyed because, looked at through the myth, all evidence supports that myth
Edward de Bono
– *pl.* clues to the spiritual potentialities of the human life
Joseph Campbell
– something that is so old that it doesn't bore you any more
Elias Canetti
– a religion in which no one any longer believes
James K Feibleman
– a moth's sister
Stan Laurel
– whatever concept or reality a whole people has arrived at over years of observation
Toni Morrison
– the presentation of facts belonging to one category in the idioms belonging to another
Gilbert Ryle
(see also *legend*)

mythology – the womb of man's initiation to life and death
Joseph Campbell

n

nagging – constructive criticism too frequently repeated
Percy Cudlipp
– the repetition of unpalatable truths
Edith Summerskill

nanny – someone you employ to care for your children, wash their clothes and entertain their father
Jasmine Birtles

narcissist – someone better looking than you are
Gore Vidal

narrowness – the scope of fundamentalists
Gys Miedema

nation – a society united by a delusion about its ancestry and by common hatred of its neighbours
William R Inge
– a body of people who have done great things together in the past and who hope to do great things together in the future
F H Underhill

nationalism – a silly cock crowing on its own dunghill
Richard Aldington
– the measles of the human race
Albert Einstein
– power hunger tempered by self-deception
George Orwell
– the impoliteness of the nations
Robert Sabatier

national pride – a modern form of tribalism
Robert Shnayerson

national security – the chief cause of national insecurity
Robert Anton Wilson

native – an oppressed person whose permanent dream is to become the persecutor
Frantz Fanon

natural selection – a mechanism for generating an exceedingly high degree of improbability
Ronald Fisher

natural birth control – showing your husband the contents of your first child's nappy
Jasmine Birtles

nature – only an immense ruin
Paul Claudel
– that lovely lady to whom we owe polio, leprosy, smallpox, syphilis, tuberculosis and cancer
Stanley N Cohen

naturist holiday – holiday where loss of luggage by airline presents no great problem
Mike Barfield
(see also *good holiday, holiday, vacation*)

Navy – a master plan designed by geniuses for execution by idiots
Herman Wouk

Nebraska – proof that Hell is full and the dead are walking the earth
Liz Winstead

necessity – the mother of convention
John S Crosbie
– the smotherer of convention
Lambert Jeffries
– the mother of taking chances
– the mother of attraction
Luke McKissack

neighbour – the best part of a real estate bargain
Austin O'Malley

nerve – what we live on, after our nerves are shot
Mignon McLaughlin

net – the biggest word in the language of business
Herbert Casson

nettle – the mosquito of the plant world
Lévi Weemoedt

network – what fishermen do when not fishing
Peter Darbo

neurosis – a substitute for legitimate suffering
Carl G Jung
– the way of avoiding non-being by avoiding being
Paul Tillich
– a secret you don't know you're keeping
Kenneth Tynan

neurotic – someone who can go from the bottom to the top, and back again, without ever once touching the middle
Mignon McLaughlin

neutron bomb – a particularly thoughtful and ingenious weapon, capable of killing people without the inconvenience of destroying property
Edmund H Volkart
(see also *atom bomb, tactical nuclear weapon*)

never – a ridiculous word you should *never* use
Simon Carmiggelt
– a long, long word, but it's less frustrating than 'God knows when'
Mignon McLaughlin
– a silly word. One can never comprehend it
Andrzej Strug

new morality – too often the old morality condoned
Hartley Shawcross

New Orleans – the only city in the world you go in to buy a pair of nylon stockings and they want to know your head size
Bill Holliday

news – the first rough draft of history
Ben Bradlee
– whatever a good editor chooses to print
Arthur McEwen
– what a chap who doesn't care much about anything wants to read
Evelyn Waugh

newspaper – a circulating library with high blood pressure
Arthur Baer
– a hideout for the frivolous
Freek de Jonge
– a device for making the ignorant more ignorant and the crazy crazier
H L Mencken
(see also *good newspaper*)

New York – the only city in the world where you can get deliberately run down on the sidewalk by a pedestrian
Russell Baker
– the only city in the world where friendliness is a felony
Milton Berle
– an exciting town where something is happening all the time, most of it unsolved
Johnny Carson
– the city of right angles and tough, damaged people
Pete Hamill
– homes, homes everywhere, and not a place to live
Don Herold
– prison towers and posters for soap and whiskey
Frank Lloyd Wright
– the nation's thyroid gland
Christopher Morley
– an unnatural city where everyone is an exile, none more so than the American
Charlotte Perkins Gilman

new york

– not Mecca, it just smells like it
Neil Simon
– home of the vivisectors of the mind
Muriel Spark
– a disco without the music
Elaine Stritch
– skyscraper National Park
Kurt Vonnegut
– the city where you can get the best cheap meal and the lousiest expensive meal in the country
Robert C Weaver
– the only place in the world where a man can be himself while working his shirt off to become somebody else
Jeanette Winterson
– a small place when it comes to the part of it that wakes up just as the rest is going to bed
P G Wodehouse

New Zealand – a country of thirty thousand million sheep – three million of whom think they are human
Barry Humphries

night-light – a safety device that allows you just enough light to see what you tripped over
Joyce Armor

Richard Nixon – a pubic hair in the teeth of America
Anon
– a man that had the morals of a private detective
William S Burroughs
– a kamikaze pilot who kept apologizing for the attack
Mary McGrory

no – the ultimate answer to all superfluous questions
Herman Brusselmans

nod – a very hip nap
Del Close

noise – what they call music in a disco bar
Jack de Graef

nonsense – an assertion of man's spiritual freedom in spite of all the oppressions of circumstance
Aldous Huxley

nonviolence – organized love
Joan Baez
– the weapon of the strong
Mahatma Gandhi

normality – a fine ideal for those who have no imagination
Carl Jung

nostalgia – a seductive liar
George Ball
– an ugly word for faithful
Herman de Coninck
– the realization that things weren't as unbearable as they seemed at the time
Heman Fay Jr
– a file that removes the rough edges from the good old days
Doug Larson
– longing for something you couldn't stand anymore
Fibber McGee
– longing for the place you wouldn't move back to
James Sanaker
– most of the time the consequence of a bad memory
Toon Verhoeven

nouvelle cuisine – a child's portion served to an adult
Henry Beard
– not enough on your plate and too much on your bill
Paul Bocuse
– roughly translated, means 'I can't believe I spent ninety-six dollars and I'm still hungry'
Mike Kalin

novel – a philosophy put into images
Albert Camus
– story that is too long and not true
Piet Grijs
– the highest example of subtle interrelatedness that man has discovered
D H Lawrence
(see also *book, detective novel, English novel, Jewish novel, literature, Russian novel*)

novelist – the historian of conscience
Frederic Raphael
(see also *author, co-author, writer*)

nowhere – a place where rest reigns
Piet Grijs

nuclear waste – something that can fade your genes
Joel Rothman

numbers – the only universal language
Nathaniel West

nutcrackers – very tight jeans
Johan Anthierens

nymphomaniac – a woman as obsessed with sex as an average man
Mignon McLaughlin
– bedseller
Hanns-Dietrich von Seydlitz
(see also *Jewish nymphomaniac*)

O

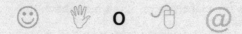

obesity – a mental state, a disease brought on by boredom and disappointment
Cyril Connolly

objective – being rational when you have nothing to lose
Colin Bowles

objectivity – subjectivity, expressed statistically
Edmund H Volkart

obscenity – such a tiny kingdom that a single tour covers it completely
Heywood Broun
– linguistic violence on the frontier of reality
Marshall McLuhan
– whatever happens to shock some elderly and ignorant magistrate
Bertrand Russell

obstacles – things a person sees when they take their mind off their goal
E Joseph Cossman

obstinacy – the energy of the stupid
Hans Habe

O Calcutta – the sort of show that gives pornography a bad name
Clive Barnes

ocean – international garbage heap
E Constant Sr
– a place where everybody is a tourist
Piet Grijs

OED database – infinite riches in a little ROM
Erich Segal

Oedipus – dilemmama
Hans-Horst Skupy

official denial – a *de facto* confirmation
John Kifner

old age – fifteen years older than I am
Bernard Baruch
– life's parody
Simone de Beauvoir
– a lot of crossed off names in your address book
Ronald Blythe
– the out-patient's department of purgatory
Robert Cecil
– that time when a man takes his teeth out more often than his wife
Ron Cichowicz
– the punishment for having lived
E M Cioran
– when most of the names in your little black book are doctors
Carolyn Coats
– when the liver spots show through your gloves
Phyllis Diller
– realizing you will never own all the dogs you wanted to
Joe Gores
– the only disease you don't look forward to being cured of
Herman J Mankiewicz
– the only thing that comes to us without effort
Gloria Pitzer
– the most unexpected of all things that happen to a man
Leon Trotsky
– a time of life when the phone rings less often, but more ominously
Edmund J Volkart
(see also *age*, *growing old*)

old people's home – the waiting-room for eternal rest
Hugo Olaerts

Olympics – the only time you can represent America and not have to carry a gun
George Raveling

ombudsman – a person hired by the governments or news organizations to deal with troublesome matters in such a manner as to justify what went wrong
Edmund J Volkart

onion – the only food-stuff that causes tears prior to being served
Henry Beard

opening night – the night before the play is ready to open
George Jean Nathan

open marriage – nature's way of telling you you need a divorce
Marshall Brickman

open mind – the gateway to heaven
Gary Barnes

open relationship – he screws around; she doesn't
Russell Ash

opera – when a guy gets stabbed in the back and instead of bleeding he sings
Ed Gardner

operation – something that takes hours to perform and years to describe
Milton Berle

opinion – the mistress of fools
W G Benham

opinion poll – a survey which claims to show what voters are thinking but which only succeeds in changing their minds
Miles Kington

opium – religion for the people
Jan Wolkers

opportunity – a bird that never perches
Claude McDonald

optimism – most often the effect of an intellectual error
Raymond Aron

– the noble temptation to see too much in everything
G K Chesterton
– the content of small men in high places
F Scott Fitzgerald
– the opium of the people
Milan Kundera
– the art of being happy with an uncertain future
Robert Sabatier

optimist – someone who does his crossword puzzle in ink
Marcel Achard
– a man who, knowing that each year was worse than the preceding, thinks next year will be better
Franklin Pierce Adams
– simply a pessimist with no job experience
Scott Adams
– a man who expects change from a taxi driver
O A Battista
– a guy who goes down to city hall to find out when his marriage license expires
Milton Berle
– the human personification of spring
Susan J Bissonette
– someone who keeps his motor running when he goes into a fashion shop with his wife
Christian Dior
– the content of small men in high places
F Scott Fitzgerald
– he that counts on others
Marcel Havrenne
– one who reckons that when his shoes wear out he will be back on his feet
Garth Henricks
– someone who believes in the Fourth World War
Gerrit Komrij
– a person who starts a new diet on Thanksgiving Day
Irv Kupcinet
– a girl who mistakes a bulge for a curve
Ring Lardner
– one who makes opportunities of his difficulties
Reginald B Mansell
– a guy that has never had much experience
Don Marquis
– a married man who wonders how he is going to spend his raise
Jacques Martain
– someone who tells you to cheer up when things are going his way
Edward R Murrow

optimist

– a fellow who believes a housefly is looking for a way to get out
George Jean Nathan
– one who believes marriage is a gamble
Laurence J Peter
– a man who hasn't got around to reading the morning papers
Earl Wilson
– a man who gets treed by a lion, but enjoys the scenery
Walter Winchell

order – the freedom offered to everyone to discover and recreate himself
Jean Genet
– merely the prevailing form of chaos
Kerry Thornley

organ – a mechanical box of whistles
Thomas Beecham

organ donor – someone who looks forward to being outlived by his liver
Rick Bayan

organic gardeners – people who till it like it is
Joel Rothman

organised crime – just the dirty side of the sharp dollar
Raymond Chandler

orgasm – when the ecstatic body grips its heaven, with little sobbing cries
E R Doods
– just one more thing to add to the average woman's guilt complex
Faith Hines

orgy – group therapy
Joey Adams
– something that looks particularly alluring seen through the mists of righteous indignation
Malcolm Muggeridge

originality – the fine art of remembering what you hear but forgetting where you heard it
Tommy Douglas
– undetected plagiarism
William R Inge
– the art of concealing your source
Franklin P Jones

orthodoxy – a corpse that doesn't know it's dead
Elbert Hubbard

ostrich – something that tastes like the progeny of an unnatural and uncomfortable liaison between a duck and a sheep
A A Gill

outer space – no place for a person of breeding
Violet Bonham Carter

outing – a nasty word for telling the truth
Armistead Maupin
– queer self-defence
Peter Tatchell

p

pacifist – someone with negative aggression
Theo A J Deddens
– a logical person who believes that since peace is so much better than war, it is not worth fighting for
Edmund J Volkart

pain – the body's way of informing the mind that we are doing something wrong, not necessarily that something is wrong
Norman Cousins
– the root of knowledge
Simone Weil

painting – a fight with yourself and the material
Karel Appel
– not a duplication of experience but the extension of experience on the plane of formal invention
Stuart Davis
– a way to forget life. It is a cry in the night. A strangled laugh
Georges Rouault

pantomime – the smell of oranges and wee-wee
Arthur Askey

papyromania – compulsive accumulation of papers
Laurence J Peter

papyrophobia – abnormal desire for 'a clean desk'
Laurence J Peter

paradise – the Luna Park of Limbo Land
Colin Bowles

paradox – a tail that eats its own snake
J Goudsblom

paragraphing – one of the lower forms of cunning, like a way with women
Harry V Wade

paranoia – negative overestimation
J A Emmens
– the erroneous belief that someone dangerous is following you, whereas we all know that it is the person ahead of you who is dangerous
Edmund J Volkart

paranoid – a man who knows a little of what's going on
William S Burroughs

paranoid-schizophrenic – someone who always thinks he is following himself
Gene Perret

parenthood – that state of being better chaperoned than you were before marriage
Marcelene Cox
– feeding the mouth that bites you
Peter De Vries
– the greatest single preserve of the amateur
Alvin Toffler

parents – the very last people who ought to be allowed to have children
Ted Bell
– people who have photos
For everyone to see
In compartments of their wallets
Where the money used to be.
Merry Browne
– people who use the rhythm method of birth control
May Flink
– the bones on which children sharpen their teeth
Peter Ustinov
(see also *first-time parents*)

Paris – the middle-aged woman's paradise
Arthur Wing Pinero

parking – street sorrow
Herb Caen

parking lot – a place where you pay to leave your car while dents are put in the fenders
Herbert V Prochnow

parking space – what disappears when you make a U-turn
Milton Berle

parkway – a place where cars are driven, as distinguished from a driveway where cars are parked
Edmund J Volkart

parliament – the longest running farce in the West End
Cyril Smith

parturition – a physiological process – the same in the countess and in the cow
W W Chipman

past– a great darkness, filled with echoes
Margaret Atwood
– a work of art, free of irrelevancies and loose ends
Max Beerbohm
– the only dead thing that smells sweet
Thomas Edward
– a foreign country; they do things differently there
L P Hartley
– a bucket of ashes
Carl Sandburg
– the present become invisible and mute
Mary Webb

pastry – the acid test of a good restaurant
Henry Root

pâté – a French meat loaf that's had a couple of cocktails
Carol Cutler

pathos – the laziness of logic
Hans Kasper

patience – virtue that one has to have in order to learn it
Karel Boullart
– something that often gets the credit that belongs to fatigue
Franklin P Jones

– the virtue most needed just when we run out of it
Alfredo La Mont
– something you admire in the driver behind you and scorn in the one ahead
Mac McCleary
– the ability to put up with people you'd like to put down
Ulrike Ruffert

patio – what your husband calls the back part of your house since the walls collapsed
Cy DeBoer

patriotism – the first bolt-hole of the hypocrite
Melvyn Bragg
– an arbitrary veneration of real estate above principles
George Jean Nathan
– the last refuge of the sculptor
William C F Plomer
– the love of a monkey for its fatherland
Alexander Pola
– the willingness to kill and be killed for trivial reasons
Bertrand Russell
– a pernicious, psychopathic form of idiocy
– your conviction that this country is superior to all other countries because you were born in it
George Bernard Shaw

peace – break between two wars
Lu Hsün
– a more toilsome business than war, at least for anyone who does not himself need to fight in a war
Murray Kempton
– a continuation of war by other means
Vo Nguyen Giap
– when time doesn't matter as it passes by
Maria Schell
– the safety valve of the world history
Hans-Horst Skupy
– the one condition of survival in this nuclear age
Adlai Stevenson

pearl – an oyster tumour
Colin Bowles

pedagogue – a monster with teeth of chalk
Jeroen Brouwers

pedantry – the dotage of knowledge
Holbrook Jackson

pedestal – as much a prison as any small space
Gloria Steinem

pedestrian – a man with two cars, a wife, and a son
Milton Berle
– someone who is looking for his car
Frédéric Dard
– a man whose son is home from college
Maxim Drabon
– anyone who is knocked down by a motor car
J B Morton

peeping tom – a guy who is too lazy to go to the beach
Henny Youngman

pekes – biological freaks
E B White

penis – obviously going the way of the veriform appendix
Jill Johnston

Pentagon – immense monument to modern man's subservience to the desk
Oliver Shewell Franks

peptic ulcer – a hole in a man's stomach through which he crawls to escape from his wife
J A D Anderson

perennial – a flower that continues to live after it dies
Art Linkletter

perfectionist – someone who looks for the hole in a transparent window
Gys Miedema

perfect lover – one who turns into a pizza at 4.00 a.m.
Charles Pierce
(see also *lover*)

perfect politician – a person who can lie to the press, then believe what he reads
Will Durst

perfect wife – one who doesn't expect a perfect husband
Anon
(see also *ideal wife, modern wife, wife*)

period – the end of a grammatical sentence and the beginning of a woman's sentence
Cy DeBoer

permissiveness – removing the dust sheets from our follies
Edna O'Brien
– neglect of duty
Zig Ziglar

perseverance – the hard work you do after you get tired of doing the hard work you already did
Newt Gingrich

personal injustice – a stronger motivation than any instinct for philanthropy
John Irving

personality – everything that's false in a human, everything that's been added on to him and contrived
Sam Shepard

perversity – the muse of modern literature
Susan Sontag

pessimism – a luxury a Jew can never allow himself
Golda Meir
– the wisdom of the experienced
Alexander Pola
– hobby with which the neighbours have most of the fun
Julien de Valckenaere

pessimist – a man who was positive nobody would gave him any ties for Christmas
O A Battista
– someone who worked with an optimist for three months
Robert Beauvais
– a man who thinks that God created the earth in six days and then was laid off
Milton Berle
– someone who only sees the sunstrokes
Karel Boullart
– someone who, if he is in the bath, will not get out to answer the telephone
Quentin Crisp

– a person who mourns the future
Isabelle C Dickson
– someone who regrets what he is about to do
J Goudsblom
– one who makes difficulties of his opportunities
Reginald B Mansell
– a person who has had to listen to too many optimists
Don Marquis
– someone who regrets it when optimists are right
Jean Marsac
– a man who looks both ways when he's crossing a one-way street
Laurence J Peter
– a man who knows the next year can't be any worse than the last one
Franklin Pierce Adams
– an optimist with a sense of reality
Alexander Pola
– someone who is pleased with bad experiences, because they prove he is right
Heinz Rühmann
– a man who thinks everybody is as nasty as himself and hates them for it
George Bernard Shaw
– an optimist on his way home from the race track
Red Smith

petition – a list of people who didn't have the courage to say no
Evan Esar

phallocrat – name the impotents give to normal people
Georges Elgozy

Philadelphia – a metropolis sometimes known as the City of Brotherly Love, but more accurately as the City of Bleak November Afternoons
S J Perelman

philanthropist – one who gives away what he should give back
Joey Adams

philosopher – *pl.* adults who persist in asking childish questions
Isaiah Berlin
– the cartographer of human life
René Daumal
– someone who can be silent in different languages
Eugeniusz Iwanicki

philosopher

– one who loves wisdom but whose love is usually unrequited
L A Rollins
– one who has a problem for every solution
Robert Zend

philosophise – only another way of being afraid and leads hardly anywhere but to cowardly make-believe
Louis-Ferdinand Céline

philosophy – the purple bullfinch in the lilac tree
T S Eliot
– finding bad reasons for what one believes for other bad reasons
Aldous Huxley
– systematic reflection upon the common experience of mankind;
Robert Maynard Hutchins
– looking at things which one takes for granted and suddenly seeing that they are very odd indeed
Iris Murdoch
– the replacement of category-habits by category-disciplines
Gilbert Ryle
– the product of wonder
A N Whitehead
– a struggle against the bewitching of our minds by means of language
Ludwig Wittgenstein

photograph – a brothel without walls
Marshall McLuhan
– *pl.* pictures taken to please the family, bore the neighbors, and enrich the camera shops
Edmund J Volkart

photography – a tool for dealing with things everybody knows about but isn't attending to
Emmet Gowin
– focus pocus
Terrance Hughes
– the uppity housemaid of painting
Janet Malcolm
– the 'art form' of the untalented
Gore Vidal

physicists – the Peter Pans of the human race. They never grow up, they keep their curiosity
I I Rabi

physics – the universe's operating system
Steven R Garman

picnic – a meal eaten more than 50 yards from the nearest toilet
Henry Beard
– a meal of tinned food eaten in a motor car by the roadside
J B Morton

pier – a disappointed bridge
James Joyce

pigeon – rat with wings
Alfred Small

pillage – to plunder a pharmacy
Johnny Hart

pink elephant – a beast of bourbon
John S Crosbie

pirouette – a whirlwind made to measure
Gys Miedema

pity – the deadliest feeling that can be offered to a woman
Vicki Baum

plagiarism – the only 'ism' Hollywood believes in
Dorothy Parker

planned economy – where everything is included in the plans except economy
Carey McWilliams
(see also *economy*)

planning – another word for the vision that sees a creative achievement before it is manifest
James L Pierce

platitude – a truth repeated until people get tired of hearing it
Stanley Baldwin

platonic friendship – the interval between the introduction and the first kiss
Sophie Irene Loeb
– the story a woman puts up to a man before, and to the world afterwards
Sidney Tremayne
– euphemism for lack of courage
Herluf van Merlet
(see also *friendship*)

platonic love – being invited into the wine cellar for a sip of pop
Anon
– love from the neck up
Thyra Samter Winslow
(see also *art of love, eternal love, fall in love, first love, ideal love, love, true love*)

play – the exultation of the possible
Martin Buber
– work that you enjoy doing for nothing
Evan Esar

playboy – a man who comes to work from a different direction every morning
L L Levinson

playful toddler – a groin-seeking missile
Jasmine Birtles
(see also *three-year-old child, toddler*)

pleasure – the best compliment
Coco Chanel

plumber – an adventurer who traces leaky pipes to their source
Arthur Baer

plus sign – the crucifix of capitalism
Guy Commerman

poem – a form of refrigeration that stops language going bad
Peter Porter
(see also *good poem, literature, poetry*)

poet – a person who is passionately in love with language
W H Auden
– a liar who always speaks the truth
Jean Cocteau
– a parrot that repeats what is never said
Stanislaw Jerzy Lec
– *pl.* the most practical people on earth so long as they are allowed to do what they like
Eric Linklater
– a sculptor that paints music
Clem Schouwenaars
– the priest of the invisible
Wallace Stevens
(see also *writer*)

poetry – the only art people haven't yet learned to consume like soup
W H Auden
– music made less abstract
Imanu Baraka
– the only means of putting a tolerable order upon the emotions
R P Blackmur
– the impish attempt to paint the color of the wind
Maxwell Bodenheim
– the result of a struggle in the poet's mind between something he wants to say and the medium in which he is trying to say it
Gerald Brenan
– life distilled
Gwendolyn Brooks
– one word leading to another
C Buddingh'
– an act of affirmation. I affirm I live, I do not live alone
Remco Campert
– a religion without hope
Jean Cocteau
– emotion recollected in a highly emotional state
Wendy Cope
– language at its most distilled and most powerful
Rita Dove
– a sport for idiots
T S Eliot
– ordinary language raised to the *n*th power
Paul Engle
– what gets lost in translation
Robert Frost
– the language in which man explores his own amazement
Christopher Fry
– the fifth point of the compass
Jan Greshoff
– an impassioned testament to man's inner freedom
Shiv Kumar
– what Milton saw when he went blind
Don Marquis
– the Cinderella of the Arts
Harriet Monroe
– the mysteries of the irrational perceived through rational words
Vladimir Nabokov
– adolescence fermented, and thus preserved
José Ortega Y Gasset
– a criticism of life in terms of beauty
Mrs George Pierce
– an evasion of the real job of writing prose
Sylvia Plath

– the revelation of a feeling that the poet believes to be interior and personal which the reader recognizes as his own
Salvatore Quasimodo
– a perfectly possible means of overcoming chaos
I A Richards
– a language that tells us, through a more or less emotional reaction, something that cannot be said
E A Robinson
– the language that is hidden behind the language
Robert Sabatier
– the achievement of the synthesis of hyacinths and biscuits
Carl Sandburg
– what makes the invisible appear
Nathalie Sarraute
– the deification of reality
Edith Sitwell
– a search for the inexplicable
Wallace Stevens
– statements on the way to the grave
Dylan Thomas
– trouble dunked in tears
Gwyn Thomas
– simply literature reduced to the essence of its active principle
Paul Valéry
(see also *blank verse, good poem, literature*)

poise – the ability to keep on talking while the other guy reaches for the check
Milton Berle

polar exploration – the cleanest and most isolated way of having a bad time which has been devised
Apsley Cherry-Garrard

politeness – the most explicit form of despite
Heinrich Böll
– the small print of the Ten Commandments
Godfried Bomans
– cosmetics of the hypocrite
Alexis Devillé
– not speaking evil of people with whom you have just dined until you are at least a hundred yards from their house
André Maurois
– one half good manners and the other half good lying
Mary Wilson Little

political convention – a chess tournament disguised as a circus
Alistair Cooke

political correctness – censorship under another name
Peter Hall

political history – far too criminal a subject to be a fit thing to teach children
W H Auden
(see also *history, human history*)

political oratory – the art of saying platitudes with courtesy and propriety
Armando Palacio Valdés

political problem – an economical problem without a solution
Georges Elgozy

political war – one in which everyone shoots from the lip
Raymond Moley
(see also *war*)

politician – a person who can make waves and then make you think he's the only one who can save the ship
Ivern Ball
– an acrobat that keeps his balance by saying the opposite of what he does
Maurice Barrès
– a man who can straddle the fence while he keeps both ears to the ground
Milton Berle
– an arse upon which everyone has sat except a man
e e cummings
– a man who can be verbose in fewer words than anyone else
Peter De Vries
– a fellow who will lay down your life for his country
Texas Guinan
– someone who speaks twice before he thinks
Tom Lanoye
– a person with whose politics you don't agree; if you agree with him he is a statesman
David Lloyd George
– any citizen with influence enough to get his old mother a job as a charwoman in the City Hall
H L Mencken
– *pl.* a number of anxious dwarfs trying to grill a whale
J B Priestley

– *pl.* are people who, when they see the light at the end of the tunnel, order more tunnel
John Quinton
– a statesman who approaches every problem with an open mouth
Adlai Stevenson
– a man who expects us to keep his promises
Jan Vanspauwen
– someone who will always be there when he needs you
Ian Walsh
(see also *good politician, honest politician, perfect politician, statesman, successful politician*)

politics – the gentle art of getting votes from the poor and campaign funds from the rich, by promising to protect each from the other
Oscar Ameringer
– a thing that only the unsophisticated can really go for
Kingsley Amis
– the balancing of unpleasant alternatives
Octavius Apple
– show business for ugly people
Paul Begala
– the art of looking for trouble, finding it whether it exists or not, diagnosing it incorrectly and applying the wrong remedy
Ernest Benn
– a blood sport
Aneurin Bevan
– the executive expression of human immaturity
Vera Brittain
– the art of the possible
R A Butler
– is not the art of the possible. It consists in choosing between the disastrous and the unpalatable
J K Galbraith
– the art of acquiring, holding and wielding power
Indira Gandhi
– too serious a matter to be left to the politicians
Charles de Gaulle
– the art of achieving the maximum amount of freedom for individuals that is consistent with the maintenance of social order
Barry Goldwater
– word derived from the word ‘poly’ meaning ‘many’, and the word ‘ticks’ meaning ‘blood sucking parasites’
Larry Hardiman
– the science of how who gets what, when and why
Sidney Hillman
– a derby of Trojan horses
Stanislaw Jerzy Lec

– the art of transforming deeds into words
Karel Jonckheere
– who gets what, when, how
Harold Lasswell
– a form of astrology – and money is its sign
John Leonard
– the art of looking for trouble, finding it, misdiagnosing it and then misapplying the wrong remedies
Groucho Marx
– to use expensive words to describe cheap remarks
Wim Meyles
– the art of helping oneself to people
Henri de Montherlant
– the diversion of trivial men who, when they succeed at it, become important in the eyes of more trivial men
George Jean Nathan
– the art of making it sound as if Santa Claus comes in November
Russell Newbold
– a lousy way for a free man to get things done
P J O'Rourke
– the skilled use of blunt objects
Lester Pearson
– a male invention that emphasises conflict and confrontation
Tom Peterson
– the second oldest profession that bears a very close resemblance to the first
Ronald Reagan
– that what is based on the indifference of the majority
James Reston
– war without bloodshed
Mao Tse-Tung
– the art of preventing people from taking part in what properly concerns them
Paul Valéry
– the art of making the inevitable possible
Gaby vanden Berghe
– the art of making believe that the other party is lying
René Vermandere
– the deliberate use of words not for communication but to screen intention
Gore Vidal
– the entertainment branch of industry
Frank Zappa
(see also *art of politics*)

pollution – the contamination of Mother Nature by human nature
Joel Rothman
(see also *water pollution*)

pop art – the indelible raised to the unspeakable
Leonard Baskin

popcorn – the last area of the movie business where good taste is still a concern
Mike Barfield

pop culture – a culture of accessible fantasy
Margot Hentoff

pop music – rock music without the sex or the soul
Mark Fisher
– the classical music of now
Paul McCartney
(see also *music*)

popularity – the capacity for listening sympathetically when men boast of their wives and women complain of their husbands
H L Mencken

pornography – the attempt to insult sex
D H Lawrence
– one of the branches of literature – science fiction is another – aiming at disorientation, at psychic dislocation
Susan Sontag

port – the milk of donhood
Max Beerbohm

portrait – a picture in which there is something wrong with the mouth
Eugene Speicher

possess – a verb, invented by people who are bored
Chris Yperman

possession – friendship between men and things
Jean-Paul Sartre

possibly – no in three syllables
L L Levinson

posterity – the patriotic name for grandchildren
Art Linkletter

post office – the old stamping grounds
Fibber McGee

postwar architecture – the accountants' revenge on the prewar businessmen's dreams
Rem Koolhaas
(see also *architecture*)

potato – an Irish avocado
Fred Allen
– the only good thing ever to come from America
N F Regnault

poverty – having enough money to buy all the things you ever wanted to have if only you hadn't got children
Jasmine Birtles

power – something of which I am convinced there is no innocence this side of the womb
Nadine Gordimer
– the ability not to have to please
Elizabeth Janeway
– the ultimate aphrodisiac
Henry Kissinger

power politics – the diplomatic name for the law of the jungle
Ely Culbertson

practice – the only norm for verifying truth
Deng Xiaoping

prayer – the most odious of concealed narcissisms
John Fowles
– the key of the morning and the bolt of the evening
Mohandas K Gandhi

preamble – warm-up before a walk
Ray Hand

preconceived notions – the locks on the door to wisdom
Merry Browne

pregnancy – a time when you realise just how pointless a man's existence is in the grand scheme of things
Jasmine Birtles

pregnant – full of love
Johan Anthierens

prejudice – a device enabling you to form opinions without getting the facts
Robert Quillen

première – a large number of people standing around looking famous
Dennis Mackail

present – the point at which time touches eternity
C S Lewis
– the history of the future
Alexander Pola

prestige – the shadow cast by power
Dean Acheson

pride – a luxury a woman in love can't afford
Clare Booth Luce
– no match for dirty diapers
James J Griffitts
– a weak spine for a straight back
Gys Miedema
– a tricky, glorious, double-edged feeling
Adrienne Rich

prime time – the precious evening hours of our lives that most of us spend watching television
Rick Bayan

primitive artist – an amateur whose work sells
Grandma Moses

Princess Margaret – the Billy Carter of the British monarchy
Robert Lacey

principles – a dangerous form of social dynamite
Katherine Susan Anthony

prison – a guest house with so many amenities that many of its patrons are quite happy to return
Lambert Jeffries

prisoner of war – a man who tries to kill you and fails, and then asks you not to kill him
Winston Churchill

privacy – keeping taboos in their place
Kate Millett

private property – the original source of freedom. It still is its main bulwark
Walter Lippmann

PR man – a press agent with a manicure
Alan Gordon

problem – *pl.* chances for you to do your best
Duke Ellington
– *pl.* opportunities in work clothes
Henry Kaiser
– *pl.* opportunities with thorns on them
Hugh Miller
– something you have hopes of changing. Anything else is a fact of life
C R Smith
– a solution in disguise
M N Teerenstra

procrastination – the wave of the future
Octavius Apple
– the thief of time
John Dos Passos
– the art of keeping up with yesterday
Don Marquis

procurer – fornicaterer
Joey Adams

prodigy – a child who plays the piano when he ought to be in bed
J B Morton
– a child who knows as much when it is a child as it does when it grows up
Will Rogers

producer – a man who is there long before the shooting starts, and way after the shooting stops
Julia Phillips
(see also *associate producer*, *cinema*, *film*, *Hollywood*)

profanity – a man's way of letting off scream
O A Battista

professional – someone who can do his best work when he doesn't feel like it
Alistair Cooke

professional football – the primary cause of wife abandonment by modern males, who sit spellbound before the tube as teams of hulks try to outdo each other in offensiveness
Rick Bayan
(see also *football*)

professional writer – an amateur who didn't quit
Richard Bach
(see also *author, co-author, freelance writer, novelist, screenwriter, writer*)

professor – one who talks in someone else's sleep
W H Auden
– a gentleman who has a different opinion
August Bier

profitability – the sovereign criterion of the enterprise
Peter Drucker

profits – part of the mechanism by which society decides what it wants to see produced
Henry C Wallich

progress – the injustice one generation passes on to the previous
E M Cioran
– a comfortable disease
e e cummings
– the exchange of one nuisance for another nuisance
Havelock Ellis
– man's ability to complicate simplicity
Thor Heyerdahl
– is stepping in dogshit and putting it down to experience
John Lennon
– a line through a list
L D McClanahan
– a gradual discovery that man's questions have no meaning
Antoine de Saint-Exupéry

promiscuous person – someone who is still thinking of sex when you don't anymore
Philippe Bouvard
– someone who is getting more sex than you are
Victor Lownes

promoters – guys with two pieces of bread looking for a piece of cheese
Evel Knievel

promotion – new title, new salary, new office, same old crap
Robert Barron & Jim Fisk

propaganda – a monologue which seeks not a response but an echo
W H Auden
– that branch of the art of lying which consists in nearly deceiving your friends without quite deceiving your enemies
Frances C D Cornford
– a seeding of the self in the consciousness of others
Elizabeth Drew
– the art of persuading others of what one does not believe oneself
Abba Eban
– what education is called if it's on behalf of an unpopular cause
Edmund J Volkart

prophecy – a poor substitute for experience
Benjamin N Cardozo
– the wit of a fool
Vladimir Nabokov

prostitute – the only honest woman left in America
Ty-Grace Atkinson

proverbs – the wisdom of the streets
W G Benham

prude – one who is troubled by improper thoughts, as distinguished from the rest of us, who rather enjoy them
Babe Webster

prudent investor – someone who made money in the third quarter
Kurt Brouwer

prune – a plum that hasn't taken care of itself
Art Linkletter

psychiatrist – the next man you start talking to after you start talking to yourself
Fred Allen
– a fellow who asks you a lot of expensive questions your wife asks you for nothing
Sam Bardell
– a person who owns a couch and charges you for lying on it
Edwin Brock
– a person who studies the problems of others in an attempt to understand his own problems
Leonard Rossiter

psychiatrist

– a man who goes to the Folies-Bergère and looks at the audience
Mervyn Stockwood
– a Jewish doctor who can't stand the sight of blood
Henny Youngman
(see also *honest psychiatrist*)

psychiatry – the care of the id by the odd
Anon
– spending 50 dollars an hour to squeal on your mother
Mike Connolly
– the art of teaching people how to stand on their own feet while reclining on couches
Shannon Fife
– science that enables us to correct our faults by confessing our parents' shortcomings
Laurence J Peter

psychoanalysis – a wonderful discovery; it makes quite simple people feel they are complex
S N Behrman
– confession without absolution
G K Chesterton
– that mental illness which regards itself as therapy
Karl Kraus
– another method of learning how to endure the loneliness produced by culture
Philip Rieff
– where you can spend more on a couch than some people do on a six-room house
Henny Youngman

psychoanalysts – father confessors who like to listen to the sins of the fathers as well
Karl Kraus

psychologist – a man who, when a beautiful girl walks into room, watches other men's reactions
Leo Rosten

psychology – the science that tells you what you already know, in words you can't understand
Joey Adams
– the science with a long past, but only a short history
Hermann Ebbinghaus
– the theology of the twentieth century
Harry Hooton
(see also *behavioural psychology*)

psychopath – someone who lives in an ivory tower and dribbles over the battlements
Colin Bowles

psychosis – the final outcome of all that is wrong with a culture
Jules Henry

publication – the male equivalent of childbirth
Richard Ackland
– a self-invasion of privacy
Marshall McLuhan

public behaviour – merely private character writ large
Stephen R Covey

publicity – the theory that no news is bad news, that neither divorce nor adultery nor sex videotapes nor checking into a clinic to dry out will stay our celebrities from swiftly cashing in on the free exposure
Rick Bayan

public office – the last refuge of a scoundrel
Boies Penrose

public opinion – what people think people think
Frank Monaghan

public relations – the craft of arranging the truth so that people will like you
Alan Harrington
– the art of winning friends and getting people under the influence
Jeremy Tunstall

publishers – people that kill good trees to put out bad newspapers
James G Watt

puck – a hard rubber disk that hockey players strike when they can't hit one another
Jimmy Cannon

pull together – to avoid being pulled apart
Bob Allisat

pun – two strings of thought tied with an acoustic knot
Arthur Koestler
– the lowest form of humour – when you don't think of it first
Oscar Levant

punctual – childless
Joyce Armor

punctuality – a virtue, especially when your date is with a parking meter
O A Battista
– the politeness of clocks
Jean Dutourd
– the virtue of the bored
Evelyn Waugh

puritan – a person who pours righteous indignation into the wrong things
G K Chesterton
– an ox that thinks it is appalling that bulls exist
Julien de Valckenaere

puritanism – the haunting fear that someone, somewhere, may be happy
H L Mencken
– that what helps us enjoy our misery while we are inflicting it on others
Marcel Ophuls

q

QANTAS – a condom on the penis of progress
Ian Tuxworth

quantity – a very poor substitute for quality – but it's the only one around
Mignon McLaughlin

quantum particles – the dreams that stuff is made of
David Moser

quark – the sound made by an English duck
Colin Bowles

queen – often a crone on a throne
Alberto Young

question mark – a tired exclamation mark
Stanislaw Jerzy Lec

questions – the creative acts of intelligence
Frank Kingdon

quiet – what home would be without children
Peter Darbo

quotation – something that somebody said that seemed to make sense at the time
Egon J Beaudoin
– a handy thing to have about, saving one from the trouble of thinking for oneself
A A Milne
– an apt phrase or statement, never recalled until it is too late to be useful, and then attributed to the wrong source
Edmund J Volkart

quotation book – a supermarket of thoughts
Gerd de Ley

quote *v.* – to hire a text without paying rent
Karel Jonckheere

r

rabbit – the *real* fast food
Patrick de Witte

rabble – offensive term your husband uses in regard to *your* side of the family
Cy DeBoer

rabid fan – a guy who boos a television set
Jimmy Cannon

racket – a line you adopt to make money you don't deserve
John Coates

radical – anyone whose opinion differs from yours
Joey Adams
– a man with both feet firmly planted in the air
Franklin D Roosevelt
– a person whose left hand does not know what his other left hand is doing
Bernard Rosenberg

radio – a bag of mediocrity where little men with carbon minds wallow in sluice of their own making
Fred Allen
– the triumph of illiteracy
John Dos Passos
– the manly art of shouting brave words into a defenceless microphone
Peter Lind Hayes
– death in the afternoon and into the night
Arthur Miller
– all the flowing manure of the world's melody
Francis Ponge
– a creative theatre of the mind
Wolfman Jack Smith
(see also *transistor radio*)

ragtime – white music – played black
Joachim Berendt
(see also *music*)

rainbow – the apology of an angry sky
Sylvia A Voirol

raisin – a worried grape
Julian Tuwim

rap – a pounding headache set to rhythm; a profane street sermon; the end of music as we know it
Rick Bayan
– poetry set to music. But to me it's like a jackhammer
Bette Midler
(see also *music*)

rape – the only crime in which the victim becomes the accused
Freda Adler
– a conscious process of intimidation by which all men keep all women in a state of fear
Susan Brownmiller
– an act in which the genitals become a weapon
Frances Cress Welsing

rapist – a kleptomaniac of sex
Sim

reactionary – a somnambulist walking backwards
Franklin D Roosevelt

reading – to look through the eyes of an author
Okke Jager
– a means of thinking with another person's mind: It forces you to stretch your own
Charles Scribner Jr

Ronald Reagan – the Fred Astaire of foot-in-mouth disease
Jeff Davis
– the first president to be accompanied by a Silly Statement Repair Team
Mark Russell
– proof that there is life after death
Mort Sahl
– a triumph of the embalmer's art
Gore Vidal

real estate agents – God's curse on mankind when locusts are out of season
Lewis Grizzard

real friend – one who walks in when the rest of the world walks out
Walter Winchell
(see also *best friend, friend, true friend*)

real man – someone who can ski through an avalanche – and still manage not to spill any beer
Bruce Feirstein
– a creature who makes me feel that I am a woman
Elinor Glyn
(see also *male, man, modern man*)

real wealth – to afford to work without being paid
Mireille Cottenjé
(see also *wealth*)

realism – any play about depression, unemployment, or disease
Tony Dunham

realist – a guy who gives electric blankets for wedding presents
Milton Berle
– somebody who thinks the world is simple enough to be understood. It isn't
Donald Westlake

reality – may not be the best of all possible worlds but it's still the only place where you can get a decent steak
– the leading cause of stress, for those in touch with it
Woody Allen

reality

– the only word in the English language that should always be used in quotes
Anon
– an obstacle to hallucination
Anon
– that which, when you stop believing in it, doesn't go away
Philip K Dick
– something for people who cannot cope with science fiction
Guido Haas
– what's left to us after all of our failures to find it
Alan Harris
– something from which people feel the need of taking pretty frequent holidays
Aldous Huxley
– the misery claimed by the authorities
Freek de Jonge
– opium for the dreamers
Marcel Mariën
– an everyday mystery
Gys Miedema
– something you rise above
Liza Minnelli
– a staircase going neither up nor down
Octavio Paz
– a weird dream
Hugo Raes
– what you step in when your head is in the clouds
Philip Simborg
– an illusion created by a lack of alcohol
N F Simpson
– nothing but a collective hunch
– a crutch for people who can't cope with drugs
Lily Tomlin
– something the human race doesn't handle very well
Gore Vidal
– the best kind of satire
Vladimir Vojnovitsj
– the leading cause of stress for those in touch with it
Jane Wagner
– only a Rorschach ink-blot
Alan Watts

reason – an emotion for the sexless
Heathcote Williams

rebel – a man who says no
Albert Camus

receiver – someone appointed by the court to take what's left
Robert Frost

reception – a sherry-go-round
Eric van der Steen

recession – what the government calls a depression that spares the rich
Rick Bayan

recipe – a series of step-by-step instructions for preparing ingredients you forgot to buy in utensils you do not own to make a dish the dog will not eat the rest of
Henry Beard

reckless motorist – man of extinction
Maxim Drabon

recycling – the meticulous separation of one's rubbish into its fundamental components, so as to conserve precious natural resources like glass and plastic
Rick Bayan

reducing diet – the taming of the chew
Shelby Friedman
(see also *diet*)

redundancy – an air-bag in a politician's car
Larry Hagman

refinance – a debt warmed up
Len Elliot

reformer – someone who will ruin the neighbour to his right just to leave a small tip for the neighbour to his left
Jan Greshoff
– a guy who rides through a sewer in a glass-bottomed boat
Jimmy Walker

refrigerator – a place where you store leftovers until they're old enough to throw out
Al Boliska

reggae music – one of them stones that was refused by the builders
Charlie Ace
(see also *music*)

regret – an appalling waste of energy
Katherine Mansfield

regulation – the substitution of error for chance
Fred J Emery

reincarnation – nothing more than the law of evolution applied to the consciousness of the individual
Sybil Leek

relics – the loose parts of a saint
Fons Jansen

religion – a desperate attempt to make ourselves believe that we don't lose our identities after we die
Octavius Apple
– an illusion that derives its strength from the fact that it falls in with our instinctual desires
Sigmund Freud
– humanity's greatest folly, greatest curse
Kevin Harris
– a defence against the experience of God
Carl Jung
– the frozen thought of men out of which they build temples
Jiddu Krishnamurti
– always a clean form of racism
Tom Lanoye
– an insurance of the present against the fire of the hereafter
Robert Lembke
– the venereal disease of mankind
Henry de Montherlant
– induced insanity
Madalyn Murray O'Hair
– a sixteenth century word for nationalism
Lewis Namier
– opium for the intellect
Leon Trotsky

remarriage – an excellent test of just how amicable your divorce was
Margo Kaufman

remorse – regret that one waited so long to do it
H L Mencken
– beholding heaven and feeling hell
George Moore

repartee – knowing what to say after you've missed your chance to
O A Battista
– what a person thinks of after he becomes a departee
Dan Bennett
– a duel fought with the points of jokes
Max Eastman

repetition – the last law of learning
John Wooden

reporter – a man who has renounced everything in life but the world, the flesh, and the devil
David Murray

Republicans – the party that says government doesn't work and then gets elected and proves it
P J O'Rourke

reputation – a bubble which a man bursts when he tries to blow it for himself
Emma Carleton
– character minus what you've been caught doing
Michael Iapoce
– what others are not thinking about you
Tom Masson
– the deepest of all masculine instincts
Virginia Woolf

research – the process of going up alleys to see if they are blind
Marston Bates
– a way of taking calculated risks to bring about incalculable consequences
Celia Green
– an organized method for keeping you reasonably dissatisfied with what you have
Charles F Kettering
– something that tells you that a mule has two ears
Albert D Lasker
– the art of the soluble
Peter Medawar
(see also *basic research*)

research men in advertising – really blind men groping in a dark room for a black cat that isn't there
Ludovic Kennedy

resemblances – the shadows of differences
Vladimir Nabokov

respect – to admire from a distance
Georges Elgozy
– the only respectable form of stupidness
Jan Greshoff

responsibility – the price every man must pay for freedom
Edith Hamilton

restaurant – public establishment where they sell indigestion
Charles Brechtspoor
(see also *great restaurants*)

résumé – a balance sheet without any liabilities
Robert Half

retire – to begin to die
Pablo Casals

retirement – twice as much husband for half as much money
Jasmine Birtles
– the time when you never do all those things you said you wanted to do if you only had the time
Ron Cichowicz
– one sure way of shortening life
Frank Conklin
– the ugliest word in the language
Ernest Hemingway
– when the living is easy and the payments are hard
Robert Orben
(see also *early retirement*)

retro-style – last refuge in case of a lack of imagination
Robert Sabatier

reunions – the conveyor belts of our individual histories
Alex Haley

revelation – the daughter of refusal
André Breton

revenge – a dish which people of taste prefer to eat cold
Dennis Price

reviewmanship – to show that it is really you yourself who should have written the book, if you had had the time
Stephen Potter
(see also *art critics, book reviewer, critic, drama critic, good critic, music critic, TV critic*)

Revised Prayer Book – an attempt to suppress burglary by legalising petty larceny
William R Inge

revolution – a struggle to the death between the future and the past
Fidel Castro
– an injustice that serves to replace as soon as possible the injustice of yesterday by the injustice of tomorrow
Jan Greshoff
– the setting-up of a new order contradictory to the traditional one
José Ortega Y Gasset
– the establishment of the future
Alexander Pola
– a trivial shift in the emphasis of suffering
Tom Stoppard
– a small stop to change drivers
Carlos de Vriese
(see also *Sexual Revolution*)

rhinoceros – an animal with a hide two feet thick, and no apparent interest in politics. What a waste
James C Wright

rich – to own too much
Frédéric Dard

rich country – a country that succeeded in hiding its poor people
Philippe Bouvard

riches – the savings of many in the hands of one
Eugene Debs

rich man – one who has succeeded in discovering that money isn't everything
O A Battista
– someone who doesn't know how poor he is
Theo Herbst

rich man

– one who isn't afraid to ask the salesman to show him something cheaper
Rita King

rich people – poor people with money
Sister Mary Tricky

right – easy to be, difficult to get, impossible to give
Piet Grijs

riot – the language of the unheard
Martin Luther King

risk – what separates the good part of life from the tedium
Jimmy Zero

road house – a place where you can fill the car and drain the family
Clyde Moore

robbery – any price charged for any article abroad
J B Norton
– redistribution of wealth
Leonard Rossiter

rock and roll – a bunch of raving shit
Lester Bangs
– music that requires very little knowledge and not much talent
Harry Connick Jr
– trying to convince girls to pay money to be near you
Richard Hell
– the hamburger that ate the world
Peter York
(see also *music*)

rock journalism – people who can't write interviewing people who can't talk for people who can't read
Frank Zappa
(see also *good journalist, investigating journalist, journalist*)

romance – the glamour which turns the dust of everyday life into a golden haze
Elinor Glyn
– the sweetening of the soul with fragrance offered by the stricken heart
Wole Soyinka
(see also *love*)

room – a place where you hide from the wolves outside
Jean Rhys

root – a flower that disdains fame
Kahlil Gibran

rose – the milk-teeth of the sun
Malcolm de Chazal
– the good conscience of its thorns
Hans Kudszus

Royal Commission – a broody hen sitting on a china egg
Michael Foot

rudeness – the weak man's imitation of strength
Eric Hoffer

rumour – a baby myth
Colin Bowles
– the only sound that is faster than light
Robert Lembke
– one thing that gets thicker as you spread it
Mary H Waldrip

rush hour – that hour when the traffic is almost at standstill
J B Morton

Russia – a riddle wrapped in a mystery inside an enigma
Winston Churchill

Russian communism – the illegitimate child of Karl Marx and Catherine the Great
Clement Attlee
(see also *communism, Bolshevism*)

Russian novel – a story in which the main character sulks for 600 pages
Colin Bowles
(see also *novel*)

rut – a grave with the ends knocked out
Laurence J Peter

S

sacrifice – a form of bargaining
Holbrook Jackson

sadist – someone who is nice to masochists
Vincent McHugh

sadness – an appetite that no misfortune can satisfy
E M Cioran
– a form of fatigue
André Gide
– twilight's kiss on earth
Wole Soyinka

safety – period in which danger takes a break
Karel Boullart

salesmanship – the difference between rape and ecstasy
Roy Herbert Thomson
(see also *successful salesman*)

sandal – shoe in a bathing-suit
Piet Grijs

San Francisco – the city that never was a town
Will Rogers
– a refugee camp for homosexuals
Carl Wittman

sanity – an illusion caused by alcohol deficiency
N F Simpson
– a cozy lie
Susan Sontag

satire – tragedy plus time
Lenny Bruce
– the weapon of the powerless against the powerful
Molly Ivins
– something that closes on Saturday night
George S Kaufman
– a grappling hook thrown up the high wall of the everyday wall
Jack Ludwig
– humour that wants to be taken seriously
Werner Mitsch

– moral outrage transformed into comic art
Philip Roth
– a back-to-front devotee
Ward Ruyslinck

satirist – a man who discovers unpleasant things about himself and then says them about other people
Peter McArthur
– the fool who sets a mousetrap to catch an elephant
Adolf Nowaczynski

Saturday – the day of the week that determines how sick a little boy was on Friday
O A Battista

save – to gather and to keep nuts till the day you have no more teeth
Jan Schepens

scandal – the manure of democracy
Dario Fo
– merely the compassionate allowance which the gay make to the humdrum
Saki
(see also *great scandal*)

scars – the definitive make-up
Herman Brusselmans

sceptic – someone who once lost his wallet in a church while standing between a policeman and a nun
Colin Bowles

scepticism – the belief of believing in nothing anymore
Julien de Valckenaere

Scheherazade – the classical example of woman saving her head by using it
Esme Wynne-Tyson

schizophrenia – illness with an even amount of patients
Piet Grijs
– a successful attempt not to adapt to pseudo-social realities
R D Laing
– a necessary consequence of literacy
Marshall McLuhan

schizophrenic – someone with two choices
Gaston Durnez

schnapps – the crack of alcohol
Denis Leary

school – *pl.* parking places for children
Greet Boon
– where you go between when your parents can't take you and industry can't take you
John Updike

school food – the piece of cod which passeth understanding
Ronald Searle & Geoffrey Williams

school run – the thirty-second dash between your illegally parked car to the school door and back again
Jasmine Birtles

school year – a long, painful period of time consisting of twenty months for students, thirty for teachers
Edmund J Volkart

science – a churchyard of hypotheses
Pierre Bourgeade
– a wonderful thing if one does not have to earn one's living at it
Albert Einstein
– the belief in the ignorance of the experts
Richard P Feynman
– any discipline in which the fool of this generation can go beyond the point reached by the genius of the last generation
Max Gluckman
– science fiction where the only boundary for your imagination is reality
Goran Hellekant
– a titanic attempt of human intellect to free itself out of its cosmic isolation by understanding
W F Hermans
– a method to keep yourself from kidding yourself
Edwin Land
– the art of systematic oversimplification
Karl Popper
– nothing but developed perception, interpreted intent, common sense rounded out and minutely articulated
George Santayana
– the refusal to believe on the basis of hope
C P Snow

– a system of exact mysteries
Jean Toomer
– a cemetery of dead ideas
Miguel de Unamuno
– a collection of successful recipes
Paul Valéry
(see also *creativity in science*)

science fiction – a kind of archaeology of the future
Clifton Fadiman

scientist – *pl.* peeping toms at the keyhole of eternity
Arthur Koestler
– *pl.* a crowd that when it comes to style and dash makes the general public look like the Bloomsbury Set
Fran Lebowitz

Scotland – land of the omnipotent No
Alan Bold

scoutmaster – an idiot dressed like a little boy, followed by little boys dressed like idiots
Maurice Biraud

screenwriter – a man who is being tortured to confess and has nothing to confess
Christopher Isherwood
– *pl.* schmucks with Underwoods
Jack Warner
(see also *author, co-author, freelance writer, professional writer, writer*)

screenwriting – an occupation akin to stuffing kapok in mattresses
S J Perelman

sculptures – mud-pies which endure
Cyril Connolly

sea horse – an embryo that gave up
Paul Rodenko

seaweed – something you don't want your neighbors to do when they look in your garden
Art Linkletter

secret – the most beautiful thing we can discover
Albert Einstein

– what you tell someone else not to tell because you can't keep it to yourself
L L Levinson
– the imitation of a mystery
Siegfried E van Praag

secret in the Oxford sense – you may tell it to only one person at a time
Oliver Shewell Franks

security – a smile from a headwaiter
Russell Baker

segregation – the offspring of an illicit intercourse between injustice and immorality
Martin Luther King

self-abuse – the devil's telephone booth
Edward Barker

self-criticism – a luxury all politicians should indulge in, but it is best done in private
Malcolm Fraser
– a mark of social maturity
Gore Vidal

self-discipline – when your conscience tells you to do something and you don't talk back
W K Hope

self-education – the only kind of education there is
Isaac Asimov

self-knowledge – a dangerous thing, tending to make man shallow or insane
Karl Shapiro

self-love – the only truthful and effective form of human love
Jan Greshoff

self-made man – one who believes in luck and sends his son to Oxford
Christina Stead

self-pity – the most destructive of the non-pharmaceutical narcotics. It is addictive, gives momentary pleasure and separates the victim from reality
John Gardner

self-respect – a question of recognising that anything worth having has its price
Joan Didion
– the secure feeling that no one, as yet, is suspicious
H L Mencken

self-righteousness – a loud din raised to drown the voice of guilt within us
Eric Hoffer

selling – essentially a transference of feeling
Zig Ziglar

sense of humour – what makes you laugh at something which would make you sore if it happened to you
Harvey Kurtzman
(see also *humour*)

sentiment – the sick half-brother of thought
Tom Lanoye

sentimentality – the sentiment we don't share
Graham Greene
– a superstructure covering brutality
C G Jung
– the emotional promiscuity of those who have no sentiment
Norman Mailer
– sentiment that rubs you up the wrong way
W Somerset Maugham
– a failure of feeling
Wallace Stevens

september – the month when a lot of people discover what a good time the moths had while they were on vacation
O A Battista

sequel – evidence that more is usually too much
Rick Bayan
– an admission that you've been reduced to imitating yourself
Don Marquis

seriousness – stupidity sent to college
P J O'Rourke

service – the rent you pay for room on this earth
Shirley Chisholm

settlement – a device by which lawyers obtain fees without working for them
D Robert White

sex – the most fun I've had without laughing
– a beautiful thing between two people. Between *five*, it's fantastic
Woody Allen
– the thing that takes up the least amount of time and causes the most amount of trouble
John Barrymore
– the liquid centre of the great New Berry Fruit of Friendship
Jilly Cooper
– the great amateur art
David Cort
– essentially just a matter of good lighting
Noel Coward
– the last refuge of the miserable
Quentin Crisp
– the invention of a very clever venereal disease
David Cronenberg
– just one damp thing after another
John S Crosbie
– God's biggest joke on human beings
– man's last desperate stand at superintendency
Bette Davis
– the Tabasco sauce which an adolescent national palate sprinkles on every course in the menu
Mary Day Winn
– the only frontier open to women who have always lived within the confines of the feminine mystique
Betty Friedan
– the best form of exercise
Cary Grant
– the gateway to life
Frank Harris
– a dirty, disgusting thing you save for somebody you love
Carol Henry
– a playground for lonely scientists
Carl Jung
– one of the most beautiful, wholesome, and natural things that money can buy
Steve Martin
– one of the nine reasons for reincarnation. The other eight are unimportant
Henry Miller
– the poor man's polo
Clifford Odets

– the mathematics urge sublimated
M C Reed
– the laughter of two bodies
Henry Root
– eroticism you can feel
Eric van der Steen
– love without wings
Hanns-Dietrich van Seydlitz
– the biggest nothing of all time
Andy Warhol
– a powerful aphrodisiac
Keith Waterhouse
– an emotion in motion
Mae West
(see also *coitus, making love*)

sex appeal – what a man can only describe with his hands
Uschi Glas
– fifty per cent what you've got and fifty per cent what people think you've got
Sophia Loren

sex drive – a physical craving that begins in adolescence and ends at marriage
Robert Byrne

sex shop – the only shop that sells parts we already have
Paul van Vliet

sexual drive – the motor memory of previously remembered pleasure
Wilhelm Reich

sexual intercourse – kicking death in the ass while singing
Charles Bukowski
– a joyous, joyous, joyous, joyous impaling of woman on man's sensual mast
Anaïs Nin

Sexual Revolution – conquest of the last frontier, involving the efficient management and manipulation of reproductive organs for the purpose of establishing the New Puritanism
Bernard Rosenberg
(see also *revolution*)

William Shakespeare – the nearest thing in incarnation to the eye of God
Laurence Olivier

shame – the feeling you have when you agree with the woman who loves you that you are the man she thinks you are
Carl Sandburg

sharing – sometimes more demanding than giving
Mary Catherine Bateson

shells – the flowers of the seabed
Jeroen Brouwers

shin – a device for finding furniture in the dark
Colin Bowles

shortcut – the longest distance between two points
Charles Issawi

show business – sincere insincerity
Benny Hill

shrink – a futile term with which to belittle a psychiatrist
Edmund J Volkart

shyness – egotism out of its depth
Penelope Keith

side effects – symptoms of a cure that induce nostalgia for the original disease
Rick Bayan

sigh – an amplifier for people who suffer in silence
Robert Orben

silence – when noise takes a nap
José Artur
– the last refuge of freedom
Michel Campiche
– argument carried on by other means
Ernesto Che Guevara
– the unbearable repartee
G K Chesterton
– the only golden thing that women don't like
Pierre Daninos
– a marvellous language that has few initiates
Roger Duhamel
– the safety zone of conversation
Arnold H Glasgow

– the prerogative of the imaginative
Georgina Hammick
– the purest speech
Alan Harris
– the world breathing
Fridal Marie Kuhlman
– the punctuation of conversation
Gys Miedema
– the only successful substitute for brains
Maurice Samuel
– the most perfect expression of scorn
George Bernard Shaw

silicone – a substance for making mountains out of molehills
Colin Bowles

simple – difficult to explain
Guy Commerman

simplicity – the quality of genius
Jan Bardi
– the peak of civilization
Jessie Sampter

sin – hoping for another life and [. . .] eluding the implacable grandeur of this life
Albert Camus
– hatred of the good for its being good
Ayn Rand
– *pl.* attempts to fill voids
Simone Weil

sink – the great symbol of the bloodiness of family life
Julian Mitchell

sitcom – what television does best: put witticisms in the mouths of performing types and remind us when to laugh
Rick Bayan

sceptic – a person who would ask God for his ID card
Edgar A Soaff

scepticism – a hedge against vulnerability
Charles Thomas Samuels

skin – that which keeps the human form in the human form
Leonard Rossiter

slang – a language that rolls up its sleeves, spits on its hands and goes to work
Carl Sandburg

sleep – an eight-hour peep show of infantile erotica
J G Ballard
– death without the responsibility
Fran Lebowitz
– our nightly bread
Ton Luiting
– an excellent way of listening to an opera
James Stephens

slot machine – the only thing that can stand with its back to the wall and defy the world
Goodman Ace

S & M – high technology sex
Pat Califia

small town – a place where everyone knows whose check is good and whose husband is not
Sid Ascher
– a place where there is little to see or do, but what you hear makes up for it
Ivern Ball
– a place where babies never arrive unexpectedly
O A Battista
– one where there is no place to go where you shouldn't
Alexander Woollcott

smell – breath's brother
Patrick Süskind

smile – the perfection of laughter
Alain
– *pl.* the soul's kisses
Minna Antrim
– a curve that sets everything straight
Phyllis Diller
– the universal welcome
Max Eastman
– an inexpensive way to improve your looks
Charles Gordy
– half a kiss
Kornel Makuszynski

– bait for a kiss
Robert Sabatier

smog – Mother Nature going prematurely grey
– the air apparent
Joel Rothman

smoking – the main cause of statistics
Fletcher Knebel

sneezing – much achoo about nothing
John S Crosbie

snobs – people that talk as if they had begotten their own ancestors
Herbert Agar
(see also *intellectual snob*)

snoring – nature's way of telling you that your spouse is still in the bed
John M Hebert

snow – powdered water
Slawomir Mrozek

soak – what tax plans may attempt to do to the rich, when the usual sources of revenue have run dry
Edmund J Volkart

soap opera – the only place in our culture where grown-up men take seriously all the things that grown-up women have to deal with all day long
Gloria Steinem

Social Democrats – the heterosexual wing of the Liberal Party
George Foulkes

socialism – Bolshevism with a shave
Anon
– the wider distribution of smoked salmon and caviar
Richard Marsh
– a system which is workable only in heaven, where it isn't needed, and in hell, where they've already got it
Cecil Palmer
– the capitalism of the lower classes
Oswald Spengler
– a fairy tale that still believes in people
Toon Verhoeven

socialist – a prim little man with a white-collar job, usually a secret teetollar and often with vegetarian leanings
George Orwell

social work – a Band-Aid on the festering wounds of society
Alexander Chase

society – public limited company with an unlimited irresponsibility
Georges Elgozy
– a self-regulating mechanism for preventing the fullfilment of its members
Celia Green
(see also *great society*)

sociologists – those academic accountants who think that truth can be shaken from an abacus
Peter S Prescott
– the astrologers and alchemists of the twentieth century
Miguel de Unamuno

sociology – the guilty science
Hortense Calisher
– the study of people who do not need to be studied by people who do
E S Turner
– using a lot of words to cover up rather obvious remarks
Barbara Wootton

sock – a highly sensitive conjugal object
Jean-Claude Kaufman

soldiers – citizens of death's grey land
Drawing no dividend from time's tomorrows.
Siegfried Sassoon

solicitor – a man who calls in a person he doesn't know to sign a contract he hasn't seen to buy property he doesn't want with money he hasn't got
Dingwall Bateson

solitude – a reward you can enjoy just by being punctual
O A Battista
– often the best society
W G Benham
– the playfield of Satan
Vladimir Nabokov

– the safeguard of mediocrity and the stern companion of genius
Dorothy Parker

solutions – the chief cause of problems
Eric Sevareid

song – the licensed medium for bawling in public things too silly or sacred to be uttered in ordinary speech
Oliver Herford
– poetry frustrated with music
Freek de Jonge

sophistication – knowing enough to keep your feet out of the crack of the theater seat in front of you
Don Herold
– understanding the difference between trinkets and treasures
Jim Rohn

sorrow – tranquillity remembered in emotion
Dorothy Parker

soul music – the way Black folks sing when they leave themselves alone
Ray Charles

space – the breath of a work of art
Frank Lloyd Wright

space travel – an extravagant feat of technological exhibitionism
Lewis Mumford
– the only presently known way of leaving this world without dying
J P Stapp

sparrow – an eagle in the eyes of a louse
Nico Scheepmaker

specialist – a doctor whose patients can be ill only during office hours
Joey Adams
– a man who fears the other subjects
Martin H Fischer
– *pl.* people who always repeat the same mistakes
Walter Gropius
– one who knows more and more about less and less
Charles H Mayo
– a doctor with a smaller practice and a bigger house
Max Tailleur

specialist

– *pl.* people who earn more and more by doing less and less
Toon Verhoeven
(see also *expert*)

speed limit – the velocity one must exceed by approximately 10 mph on a motorway or risk being run off the road
Rick Bayan

sperm bank – only a place whose come has time
Milton Berle

sperm donor – the only job for which no woman is or can be qualified
Wilma Scott Heide

spice – the plural of spouse
Christopher Morley

spinster – girl that said 'No' once too often
Raymond Peynet
– the bachelor's widow
André Prévot

spontaneity – the essence of pleasure
Germaine Greer

spook – something everyone is afraid of and no one believes in
Colin Bowles

sport – the opiate of the masses
Russell Baker
– the most unifying influence in the world today
Dennis Follows
– *pl.* the only entertainment where, no matter how many times you go back, you'll never know the ending
Gene Perret
– imposing order on what was chaos
Anthony Storr

spring – the time of youth and easy happiness
René Gysen
– nature's way of saying, 'Let's party!'
Robin Williams

stalagmites – miniature German prison guards
Spike Milligan

stale mind – the devil's breadbox
Mary Bly

stand-up comedy – the art of letting an audience laugh by simulating spontaneity
Lee Glickstein
(see also *comedy, musical comedy*)

star – just an actor who sells tickets
Charles Dance
(see also *actor, Hollywood*)

starlet – the name for any woman under thirty not actively employed in a brothel
Ben Hecht
(see also *actress, Hollywood*)

state – an instrument in the hands of the ruling class for suppressing the resistance of its class enemies
Joseph Stalin

state legislators – politicians whose darkest secret prohibits them from running for higher office
Dennis Miller

statesman – a politician who didn't get caught
Milton Berle
– a man who plays both ends against the muddle
Raymond J Cvikota
– *pl.* the word politicians use to describe themselves
Antony Jay & Jonathan Lynn
– a politician who is held upright by equal pressure from all directions
Eric A Johnston
– a politician who has been dead ten or fifteen years
Harry S Truman
– any politician it's considered safe to name a school after
Bill Vaughan
(see also *politician*)

statesmanship – housekeeping on a great scale
John Simon

statistician – a man who can use figures to support himself in a calculated manner
O A Battista

– someone who is good at figures but who doesn't have the personality to be an accountant
Roy Hyde

statistics – human beings with the tears wiped off
Paul Brodeur
– a bunch of numbers running around looking for an argument
George Burgy
– mendacious truths
Lionel Strachey

status quo – the only solution that cannot be vetoed
Clark Kerr
– Latin for the mess we're in
Jeve Moorman

Gertrude Stein – the mama of dada
Clifton Fadiman

stereo – the device teenagers use for their experiments on how many decibels it takes to reach the pain level
Joyce Armor

stiff attitude – one of the attributes of *rigor mortis*
Henry S Haskins

stockbroker – a man who can take a bankroll and run it into a shoestring
Alexander Woollcott

stopwatch – improved version of the whip
Julien Vangansbeke

straight line – a drawn out curve
Gys Miedema

stranger – just a bastard you haven't met yet
Rich Garella
– friend that you have yet to meet
Robert Lieberman

Barbra Streisand – a cross between an aardvark and an albino rat surmounted by a platinum coated horse bun
John Simon

strength – the first requirement of love
Susanna Tamaro

stress – a phenomenon generated almost exclusively by society's mad pace of the twentieth century
Barbara B Brown
– the handcuffs of the heart
Helmut Qualtinger

strip poker – the only game where the more you lose, the more you have to show for it
Henny Youngman

stripteaser – a busy body
Joey Adams

stroll – a roundabout way of arriving at a pub
Wim Kan

stupidity – intelligence cleverly disguised
Kevin A H Dean
– a character defence of turned in hostility
Paul Goodman
– a lack of capacity to take things in
Clive James
– an elemental force for which no earthquake is a match
Karl Kraus

style – primarily a matter of instinct
Bill Blass
– a simple way of saying complicated things
Jean Cocteau
– being yourself, but on purpose
Quentin Crisp
– the outer skin of your ideas
Jean Dutourd
– self-plagiarism
Alfred Hitchcock
– the hallmark of a temperament stamped upon the material at hand
André Maurois
– a word that has no plural
Auguste Perret
– knowing who you are, what you want to say, and not giving a damn
Gore Vidal

subscriber – someone who wants to read the same every morning, but on freshly printed paper
Battus

suburb – a place that isn't city, isn't country, and isn't tolerable
Mignon McLaughlin

suburbia – where the developer bulldozes out the trees, then names the streets after them
Bill Vaughan

subversive – one who doesn't like Walt Disney *or* Coca-Cola
Mignon McLaughlin

success – often a tombstone under which one gets buried alive
Bertus Aafjes
– the result of a collective hallucination stimulated by the artist
Charles Aznavour
– often the result of taking a misstep in the right direction
Al Bernstein
– the result of taking the hand you were dealt and utilizing it to the very best of your ability
Ty Boyd
– following the pattern of life one enjoys most
Al Capp
– going from failure to failure without losing enthusiasm
Winston Churchill
– a toy balloon among children armed with pins
Gene Fowler
– often only a revenge on happiness
Bernard Grasset
– the worst thing that can happen to you
Alberto Moravia
– nothing but being a quote
Andy Partridge
– the result of perfection, hard work, learning from failure, loyalty and persistence
Colin Powell
– the best revenge
Jerzy Skolimowsky
– having ten honeydew melons and eating only the top half of each one
Barbra Streisand
– having a flair for the thing that you are doing; knowing that is not enough, you have got to have hard work and a sense of purpose
Margaret Thatcher
– something your friends will never forgive you
Julian Tuwim
– often just an idea away
Frank Tyger
– place where preparation and opportunity meet
Bobby Unser

– the reward of anyone who looks for trouble
Walter Winchell

successful man – the one who finds out what is the matter with his business before his competitors do
Roy L Smith

successful politician – someone who can stand on a fence and make people believe it's a platform
(see also *politician*)

successful salesman – someone who has found a cure for the common cold shoulder
Robert Orben
(see also *salesman*)

successful tool – one that was used to do something undreamed of by its author
S C Johnson

successful woman – one who doesn't have to work as hard after marrying a man as she did trying to catch him in the first place
O A Battista
(see also *woman*)

suicide – a solution to a problem
Jean Baechler
– the only deadly sin you can never confess
François Cavanna
– the only perfect crime that remains unpunished
Warren Manzi
– no more than a trick played on the calendar
Tom Stoppard

suicide blonde – a blonde dyed by her own hand
Saul Bellow

summer colony – a place where you work hard collecting dossiers on people you don't care about
Mignon McLaughlin

sumo wrestling – survival of the fattest
Maxim Drabon

sun – the nipple in the Milky Way
Guido van Heulendonk

sunday school – a prison in which children do penance for the evil conscience of their parents
H L Mencken

sunlight – the world's best disinfectant
William Proxmire

superego – that part of the personality which is soluble in alcohol
Harold Lasswell

supermarket – a small hypermarket
Mike Barfield
– a place where you spend forty minutes looking for instant coffee
Milton Berle

superstition – someone else's religion
J C Bloem
– a premature explanation that overstays in time
George Iles
– noun accompanying the adjective medieval
J B Morton

surprise – the greatest gift which life can grant us
Boris Pasternak

surviving – being born over and over
Erica Jong

Sweden – country where they commit suicide and the king rides a bicycle
Alan Bennett

swimming pools – what children often confuse with a restroom
Joyce Armor

Switzerland – a country where few things begin, but many things end
F Scott Fitzgerald
– a small, steep country, much more up and down than sideways, and is all stuck over with large brown hotels built in the cuckoo clock style of architecture
Ernest Hemingway
– a nation of money-grabbing clockmakers
Nick Lowe
– a whole country of phobic handwashers living in a giant Barclays Bank
Jonathan Raban

symmetry – a graveyard with a British accent
Edmund J Volkart

symphony – a stage play with the parts written for instruments instead of for actors
Colin Wilson

synonym – a word you use when you can't spell the word you first thought of
Burt Bacharach

t

t – the hammer of the alphabet
Ramón Gómez de la Serna

tabloids – fast-reading for the slow thinking
Anon

tact – the rare ability to keep silent while two friends are arguing, and you know both of them are wrong
Hugh Allen
– the ability to get a barber to listen to you
O A Battista
– the art of making guests feel at home when that's really where you wish they were
George E Bergman
– simply a delicate form of lying
George A Birmingham
– knowing how far we may go too far
Jean Cocteau
– the art of recognizing when to be big and when not to belittle
Bill Copeland
– tongue in check
Sue Dytri
– the art of building a fire under people without making their blood boil
– the ability to stay in the middle without getting caught there
Franklin P Jones
– the ability to tell a man he's open-minded when he has a hole in his head
F G Kernan
– the art of convincing people that they know more than you do
Raymond Mortimer

tact

– the knack of making a point without making an enemy
Howard W Newton
– something you do not miss when you do not have it
Eric van der Steen

tactical nuclear weapon – an atomic bomb that says 'Sorry'
Battus
(see also *atom bomb, neutron bomb*)

talent – to want to do something
Jacques Brel
– one of those sad roads that lead to everywhere
André Breton
– to be amazed when you read your own writing
Gilbert Cesbron
– one muscle no one has ever over-exercised
Mignon McLaughlin

talk – sometimes a trick to say nothing
Simone de Beauvoir

talkative woman – one who [talks] as much as a man
Cheris Kramarae
(see also *woman*)

talk is cheap – assertion refuted by lawyers and mobile telephone companies
Mike Barfield

talk show – to talk bullshit with an alibi
Jan Lenferink
– an unnatural act between consenting adults in public
Michael Parkinson

tango – a sad thought to which one can dance
Edward Stachura
(see also *ballet, chat-chat-chat, dance, lambada*)

tapioca – the only known dessert that produces leftovers
Henry Beard

taste – the enemy of creativeness
Pablo Picasso

tautology – the alarm bell of the mind
Robert Sabatier

tax collector – a taxidermist who stuffs you and keeps the skin
Colin Bowles

taxes – the dues that we pay for the privileges of membership in an organized society
Franklin D Roosevelt
(see also *fair tax structure, income tax, wealth tax*)

taxi – vehicle that always seems to dissolve in the rain
Dan Bennett
(see also *cab drivers, enterprising taxi driver*)

taxpayer – someone who works for the federal government but doesn't have to take a civil service examination
Ronald Reagan

tax reform – taking the taxes off things that have been taxed in the past and putting taxes on things that haven't been taxed before
Art Buchwald

teacher – one who makes himself progressively unnecessary
Thomas Carruthers
– someone who doesn't know it either, but gets paid for it
Piet Grijs

teaching – the fine art of imparting knowledge without possessing it
Bruce W van Roy
– the greatest act of optimism
Colleen Wilcox
(see also *art of teaching, good teaching*)

tear gas – the only surefire method of getting children away from the television set
Joyce Armor

tears – one of the most potent weapons in woman's bitchy and inexhaustible arsenal
Ama Ata Aidoo
– the extinguisher for suffering
Robert Sabatier
– a sauna for the soul
Godeliva Uleners

technicality – a point of principle which we have forgotten
Elwyn Jones

technology – No Place for Wimps
Scott Adams
– a way of organizing the universe so that man doesn't have to experience it
Max Frisch

technocrat – young man with no power, who abuses it

orges Elgozy

teenager – *pl.* also known as Parent-agers
Jasmine Birtles
– stereo-type
Aldo Cammarota
– *pl.* God's punishment for having sex
Patrick Murray
– *pl.* hormones with feet
Silver Rose
(see also *adolescence*)

teeth – bars for our thoughts
E Constant Sr

telephone – the shortest way to have a long chat
Fernand Lambrecht
– a good way to talk to people without having to offer them a drink
Fran Lebowitz
– the most useful and least expensive household repair tool
Wes Smith

television – a device that permits people who haven't anything to do to watch people who can't do anything
Fred Allen
– the first truly democratic culture; the first culture available to everybody and entirely governed by what the people want. The most terrifying thing is what people do want
Clive Barnes
– the third parent
R Buckminster Fuller
– the longest amateur night in history
Robert Carson
– just one more facet of that considerable segment of our society that never had any standard but the soft buck
Raymond Chandler
– democracy at its ugliest
Paddy Chayevski
– a form of soliloquy

Kenneth Clark
– the plug-in drug
Mary Day Winn
– a medium of entertainment that permits millions of people to listen to the same joke at the same time – and yet remain lonesome
T S Eliot
– an invention whereby you can be entertained in your living room by people you wouldn't have in your house
David Frost
– a medium that has raised writing to a new low
Samuel Goldwyn
– one-eyed bandit
Piet Grijs
– the opium of the last part of the twentieth century
Larry Hagman
– the paradise of mediocrity
Toon Hermans
– a medium. So called because it is neither rare nor well done
Ernie Kovacs
– a proof that people will look at anything rather than at each other
Ann Landers
– a convenient whipping boy for the ills that afflict society
Norman Lear
– a corporate vulgarity
John Leonard
– an object proving that sight has a definite odour
Gerald F Lieberman
– chewing-gum for the eyes
Frank Lloyd Wright
– the literature of the illiterate, the culture of the low-brow, the wealth of the poor, the privilege of the underprivileged, the exclusive club of the excluded masses
Lee Loevinger
– a hole through which you push various communications
Jonathan Miller
– the entertainment which flows like tap-water
Dennis Potter
– an advanced technical method of stopping people from making their own entertainments
Leonard Rossiter
– a nightly national seance
Daniel Schorr
– the bland leading the bland
Murray Schumach
– the word is half Greek, half Latin. No good can come of it
C P Scott
– the best gauge we have of our decay

television

John Stevenson
– an ugly piece of furniture
John Walters
– the finest medium ever devised for showing old films
Keith Waterhouse
– a twenty-one-inch prison
Billy Wilder
– just media to sell goods
John Williams
(see also *cable television, commercial television, daytime TV, educational television, game show, MTV, TV, TV commercials*)

television remote control – the most effective birth control device in history
Jay Leno

television set – a machine with a picture in front; tubes in the middle; and an instalment behind
Robert Orben

tennis – a perfect combination of violent action taking place in an atmosphere of total tranquillity
Billie Jean King
– a fine balance between determination and tiredness
Virginia Wade

terrorism – the rage of literati in its last stage
Jacob Burckhardt
– armed propaganda
Frank Kitson
– propaganda by deed
Walter Laqueur
– the violence of the intelligentsia
Richard E Rubenstein

terrorist – high-minded idealist who assassinates innocent men, women and children for a good cause
Alex Ayres

Texans – proof that the world was populated by aliens
Cynthia Nelms

Margaret Thatcher – Attila the Hen
Clement Freud
– the sort of woman who wouldn't give you your ball back
Mike Harding

theatre – the first serum that man invented to protect himself from the sickness of despair
Jean-Louis Barrault
– the aspirin of the middle classes
Wolcott Gibbs
(see also *actor, actress, dinner theatre*)

theatre director – a person engaged by the management to conceal the fact that the players cannot act
James Agate

thesaurus – a dinosaur with a highly developed vocabulary
Nick Siegler

thing – a thing without a name
Marc van Halsendaele

thinking – the endeavour to capture reality by means of ideas
José Ortega Y Gasset
– the best way to travel
Michael Pinder

third world development – a cannibal using a knife
Stanislaw Jerzy Lec

thought – the sound of silence
Gys Miedema

three – an unlucky number if one is the third
Sidney Tremayne

three-year-old child – a being who gets almost as much fun out of a fifty-six-dollar set of swings as it does out of finding a small green worm
Bill Vaughan
(see also *playful toddler, toddler*)

thriller – the cardinal twentieth-century form. All it, like the twentieth century, wants to know is: Who's Guilty?
Brigid Brophy
– an extension of the fairy tale
Raymond Chandler

throat – place where lies and bread meet
Piet Grijs

thunder – the sound of God moving his beer barrels across the floor of the sky
Cyril Fletcher

thunderstorm – the rage of a god that weeps
Ben Cami

time – a dressmaker specializing in alterations
Faith Baldwin
– something you're only given when you possess so much that you don't need it
John Braine
– a River without Banks
Marc Chagall
– what one loses by trying to make a definition of it
Piet Grijs
– a circus always packing up and moving away
Ben Hecht
– the least thing we have of
Ernest Hemingway
– one-dimensional eternity
Hans Lohberger
– the coin of your life. It is the only coin you have, and only you can determine how it will be spent. Be careful lest you let other people spend it for you
Carl Sandburg
– the wealth of the poor and the poverty of the rich
Michael Schiff
– the only critic without ambition
John Steinbeck
– the longest distance between two places
Tennessee Williams
– a storm in which we are all lost
William Carlos Williams

timelessness – a watchmaker's nightmare
Gys Miedema

timer – adjustable clock that rings or otherwise signals when a particular dish is overcooked
Henry Beard

tinder – the wedding album after the divorce
Cy DeBoer

tip – a small sum of money you give to someone because you are

afraid he wouldn't like not being paid for something you haven't asked him to do
Ann B Caesar

toastmaster – the man who starts the bull rolling
Milton Berle

today – the yesterday you worried about tomorrow
Anon
– the first day of the rest of your life
C E Dederich
– the last day of the first part of your life
John Hovancsek

today's literature – prescriptions written by patients
Karl Kraus
(see also *great literature, literature*)

toddler – someone who survived the abortion wave
Jan Lambin
(see also *playful toddler, three-year-old child*)

tolerance – the ability to love people when they don't deserve it
O A Battista
– the virtue of the man without convictions
G K Chesterton
– the result of boredom
Quentin Crisp
– the positive and cordial effort to understand another's beliefs, practices, and habits without sharing or accepting them
Joshua Liebman
– another name for indifference
W Somerset Maugham

tombstone – about the only thing that can stand upright and lie on its face at the same time
Mary Wilson Little

tongue – the meanest piece of meat in the world
Jan Mens

tooth fairy – a gay dentist
Colin Bowles

topless bar – a place where you can always find a friendly face – and nobody watching it
Joey Adams

tortoise – the only animal that can make love to a hedgehog, but seldom has the urge to do that
François Cavanna

totalitarianism – the interruption of mood
Norman Mailer

tourist – someone who wants to be bored in a strange country
Karel Jonckheere

tout – a guy who has nothing to lose and makes sure you do too
Milton Berle

town – something you love when you leave it
Jos Daelman

trade – the skill of selling things before they become worthless
Jan Schepens

trade unions – islands of anarchy in a sea of chaos
Aneurin Bevan

tradition – what you resort to when you don't have the time or the money to do it right
Kurt Herbert Adler
– the democracy of the dead
W H Auden
– what provides us with the most direct access that we can have to our nature
John Benson

traditionalist – a pessimist about the future and an optimist about the past
Lewis Mumford

tragedy – situation in which both parties are right
Simon Carmiggelt
(see also *Greek tragedy*)

tramp – a ragged individualist
Jane Ace

trampoline – dance floor for optimists
Gys Miedema

transistor radio – the modern leper's bell
Ian Fleming
(see also *radio*)

translation – reproduction of Rembrandt in black and white
Johan Huizinga

travel – to discover that everyone is wrong about other countries
Aldous Huxley

tree – *pl.* the legs of the landscape
IK Bonset
– a piece of wood that can be motionless for several decades and then, one day, all of a sudden, jumps in front of your car
Françoise Sagan

trip – what you take when you can't take any more of what you've been taking
Adeline Ainsworth
– just what is needed to spoil a vacation
Edmund J Volkart

trouble – the common denominator of living. It is the great equalizer
Ann Landers

true friend – someone who never gets in your way unless you happen to be going down
Arnold H Glasgow
– one who overlooks your failures and tolerates your successes
Doug Larson
– someone who is there for you when he'd rather be anywhere else
Len Wein
(see also *best friend, friend, real friend*)

true love – when your heart and your mind are saying the same thing
Leanna L Bartram
(see also *art of love, eternal love, fall in love, first love, ideal love, love, platonic love*)

true terror – to wake up one morning and discover that your high school class is running the country
Kurt Vonnegut

trust – the best proof of love
Joyce Brothers

– the precursor to betrayal
Dave Krieger

truth – a river that is always splitting up into arms that reunite
Cyril Connolly
– what most contradicts itself
Lawrence Durrell
– the source of all lies
Alain Germoz
– the first casualty of any engagement in the battle of life
Michael Green
– a lie that is ashamed of itself
Jan Greshoff
– an argument used by people without fantasy
Henri Jeanson
– something somehow discreditable to someone
H L Mencken
– that which destroys sin
Harry Mulisch
– what we think it is at any given moment of time
Luigi Pirandello
– something so important that it needs to be surrounded by a bodyguard of lies
George Pratt Shultz
– a rare and precious commodity. We must be sparing in its use
C P Scott
– a rabbit in a bramble patch
Pete Seeger
– what one is obliged to tell policemen
Bertrand Russell
– the bottom of a bottomless well
Tennessee Williams
– a lie with long legs
Wolfram Weidner
– what we are able to believe
Eric van der Steen

t-shirts – the going form of immortality
John Crosby

tuba – the most intestinal of instruments – the very lower bowel of music
Peter de Vries

tumescence – the period between pubescence and senescence
Robert Byrne

Turkey – the mecca of the mocca
E Constant Sr

TV – a clever contraction derived from the words Terrible Vaudeville
Goodman Ace
(see also *televsion*)

TV commercials – the yak in a box
Shelly Friedman
(see also *television*)

TV critic – a man forced to be literate about the illiterate, witty about the witless and coherent about the incoherent
John Crosby
– *pl.* those who roam the channels after dark, searching for buried treasure
Harriet van Horne
(see also *critic, good critic, reviewmanship*)

twentieth-century man – one who lived within his means, but had to borrow the money to do it
Colin Bowles

u

ugliness – the safest contraceptive
Hervé Bazin
– insurance against rape
André Prévot

ukulele – the missing link between music and noise
E K Kruger

umbrella – a webbed palmtree
Piet Grijs

understand – to perceive patterns
Isaiah Berlin

understanding – the last recourse of nostalgia
Yves Bonnefoy

unfaithful – having nothing to say to your husband because you've already said everything to someone else
Françoise Sagan

unhappiness – the difference between our talents and our expectations
Edward de Bono
– not knowing what we want and killing ourselves to get it
Don Herold
– the ultimate form of indulgence
Tom Robbins

unilateral withdrawal – a concept which, if nothing else, will at least help to solve the world's population problem
Joel Rothman

United Nations – an organization for countries that cannot tolerate injustice and oppression – except at home
Joey Adams
– a temple to Parkinson's Law – where inefficiency and extravagance worship at its shrines and hypocrisy at its altars
R J D Turnbull

unity – organised hatred
John Jay Chapman

universe – merely a fleeting idea in God's mind – a pretty uncomfortable thought, particularly if you've just made a down payment on a house
Woody Allen
– all-purpose poem
Ray Hand

university – what college becomes when the faculty loses interest in students
John Ciardi
– a place where men of principle outnumber men of honor
Ernest May
– the canary in the coalmine. It is the most sensitive barometer of social change
James Perkins

unmarried man – an example of the failure of Care in the Community
Jasmine Birtles
(see also *bachelor*)

upper crust – a bunch of crumbs held together by dough
Joseph A Thomas

urinal – the one place where all men are peers
Rick Bayan

Usenet – post to exotic, distant machines. Meet exciting, unusual people. And flame them
Danny Sorensen

user – the word computer professionals use when they mean 'idiot'
Dave Barry

Utopia – that fictional wonderland where children say, 'Yes, Mother, whatever you say'
Joyce Armor
– a place where men are severely punished for all odours and noises they expel
Cy DeBoer
– what the imagination of man has to say about the possibilities of the human spirit
Howard Thurman

utter waste – a coachload of lawyers going over a cliff with three empty seats
Lamar Hunt

V

vacation – the family goes away for a rest, accompanied by mother, who sees that the others get it
Marcelene Cox
– time off to remind employees that the business can get along without them
L L Levinson
– having nothing to do and all day to do it
Robert Orben
(see also *family vacation, good holiday, holiday, naturist holiday*)

vacation time – when you spend days looking for a place to avoid next year
Milton Berle

vaccine – a microbe with its face washed
Frank Scully

vanity – other people's pride
Sacha Guitry

– the result of a delusion that someone is paying attention
Paul R Sweeney

vegetarian – someone who gives peas a chance
Colin Bowles
– a person who won't eat anything that can have children
David Brenner
– a person who won't eat meat unless someone else pays for it
Al Clethan

Venus de Milo – the goddess of disarmament
L L Levinson
– a good example of what happens to somebody who won't stop biting her fingernails
Will Rogers

veteran – old actor you thought was dead
Russell Ash

vibrator – electrical milkman
Wim de Bie & Kees van Kooten

vice – a creature of such hideous mien that the more you see it the better you like it
Finlay Peter Dunne

vice president – someone who presides over the Senate and sits around hoping for a funeral
Harry S Truman

vicious circle – the one and only perpetuum mobile
Marie Claire Loupard

Victorian apartment – place where the bedrooms have only enough space for one tightly bound woman
Wes Smith

village – part of the churchyard where the living rest
Julien de Valckenaere

villains – people who do the same things that we do, but we have the right reasons
Mignon McLaughlin

viola – the hermaphrodite of the orchestra
Thomas Beecham

violence – the last refuge of the incompetent
Isaac Asimov
– one of the biggest industries in America
Alain Bosquet
– the repartee of the illiterate
Alan Brien
– the Sphinx by the Fireside, and she has a human face
Jacob Bronowski
– man re-creating himself
Frantz Fanon
– the way of ensuring a hearing for moderation
William C O'Brien
– a sign of weakness
Dominique Rocheteau

virgin – no man's land
Karel Jonckheere

virginity – a big issue about a little issue
Milton Berle

virility – an illness which is best avoided
Nicholas Goodison

virtue – the failure to achieve vice
John C Armor
– consists in avoiding scandal and venereal diseases
Robert Cecil
– the vice of the majority
Jean Genet
– its own revenge
E Y Harburg

vitality – the pursuit of life
Katharine Hepburn

voice – a second face
Gérard Bauer

voice mail – the technological upchuck of the age
Herb Caen

voluptuous woman – one who has curves in places where some girls don't even have places
Henny Youngman
(see also *woman*)

voting – a civic sacrament
Theodore Hesburgh
– a way of determining which side is the stronger without putting it to the test of fighting
H L Mencken
– a process of standing in line to decide which party will waste your money
Babe Webster

vulgarity – the garlic in the salad of taste
Cyril Connolly

W

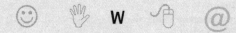

wages – the measure of dignity that society puts on a job
Johnnie Tillmon

Wagner – the Puccini of music
J B Morton

waist – a terrible thing to mind
Tom Wilson

Waiting For Godot – a play in which nothing happens, twice
Vivian Mercier

walking – what parents always did as children to get to school, further than anyone else, through more snow, up more hills and with more joy and gratitude
Jasmine Birtles

want – to have a weakness
Margaret Atwood

war – a luxury that only small nations can afford
Hannah Arendt
– a highly co-operative method and form of theft
Jacob Bronowski
– little more than a catalogue of mistakes and misfortunes
Winston Churchill
– for some a *via dolorosa*, for others a *via* dollar*osa*
Zygmunt Fijas
– a temporary misunderstanding
Wim Kan
– a cowardly escape from the problems of peace
Thomas Mann

– God's way of teaching us geography
Paul Rodriguez
– capitalism with the gloves off
Tom Stoppard
– the unfolding of miscalculations
Barbara Tuchman
– an organized bore
Oliver Wendell Holmes Jr
– fear cloaked in courage
William Westmoreland
(see also *political war*)

war between the sexes – the only one in which both sides regularly sleep with the enemy
Quentin Crisp

Washington – a much better place if you are asking questions rather than answering them
John Dean
– a steering wheel that's not connected to an engine
Richard Goodwin
– an endless series of mock palaces clearly built for clerks
Ada Louise Huxtable
– a city of Southern efficiency and Northern charm
John F Kennedy
– a place where politicians don't know which way is up and taxes don't know which way is down
Robert Orben
– the only place where sound travels faster than light
Carl Thompson

Watergate – clear proof of the fact that when it comes to ingenuity the human mind is at its best trying to cover things up
O A Battista
– the only brothel where the madam remained a virgin
Mort Sahl
– a notorious political scandal that pulled a President of the United States down and investigative reporting up
Edmund J Volkart

water pollution – cirrhosis of the river
Joel Rothman
(see also *pollution*)

wealth – the product of man's ability to think
Ayn Rand
(see also *real wealth*)

wealth tax – capital punishment
Leonard Rossiter
(see also *fair tax structure, income tax, taxes*)

wedding – a funeral where you smell your own flowers
Eddie Cantor
– a necessary formality before securing a divorce
Oliver Herford
– the point at which a man stops toasting a woman and begins roasting her
Helen Rowland
(see also *marriage*)

wedlock – the deep, deep peace of the double bed after the hurly-burly of the *chaise longue*
Mrs Patrick Campbell

weed – a plant with nine lives
Milton Berle
– a plant with a star of David
J C F Kessler
– simply a plant that you don't want
John Simmons

well-adjusted person – one who makes the same mistake twice without getting nervous
Jane Heard

well-being – productivity plus justice
Helmut Nahr

well-timed silence – the most commanding expression
Mark Helprin

Mae West – a plumber's idea of Cleopatra
W C Fields

wheel – man's greatest invention until he got behind it
Bill Ireland
– *pl.* the thoughts of legs
Harry Mulisch

whining – anger through a small opening
Stephen Stewart Smalley

whiskey – the most popular of the remedies that won't cure a cold
Jerry Vale

White House – the finest jail in the world
Harry S Truman

whore – a mother with a cunt
Jan Wolkers

widow – a girl that has nothing to fear anymore
Robert de Flers
(see also *grass widow*)

widower – the only man who can make more money than his wife can spend
O A Battista

widowhood – the only good thing some women get out of marriage
Jasmine Birtles

wife – somebody you make love to so you can get the cooking and cleaning done
Milton Berle
– the wind beneath a man's wings
Bill Cosby
– *pl.* people who think it's against the law not to answer the phone when it rings
Ring Lardner
– a former sweetheart
H L Mencken
– *pl.* people who feel they don't dance enough
Groucho Marx
(see also *housewife, ideal wife, modern wife, perfect wife*)

will – the only means the dead have to take revenge on the living
André Prévot
– the most loved of all literature
Wolfram Weidner

willpower – being able to eat just one salted peanut
Pat Elphinstone

wind – the only thing in civilization to enjoy freedom
Elias Canetti

Word for Windows – for some people it's an operating system – for others the longest exe-file in the world
Anon

windscreen wipers – the eyelashes of rain
Johan Anthierens

wine – the Mozart of the mouth
Gérard Depardieu
– the juice of the grape gone bad
Donald Soper
(see also *Beaujolais*)

wings – a poor substitute for thrust
Alan Anderson

wink – a temptation in rompers
O A Battista

winner – someone who recognizes his God-given talents, works his tail off to develop them into skills, and uses these skills to accomplish his goals
Larry Bird

winter – nature's way of saying, 'Up yours'
Robert Byrne

wisdom – knowing when you can't be wise
Paul Engle
– the reward you get for a lifetime of listening when you'd have preferred to talk
– the quality that keeps you from getting into situations where you need it
Doug Larson
– a spiritual greed
V S Pritchett
– deepest platitude
Gore Vidal

wisecracking – calisthenics with words
Dorothy Parker

wish – the enemy of happiness
Ton Luiting
– the mother of disappointment
Alexander Pola

wit – the only wall
        Between us and the dark
Mark Van Doren

woman – the future of man
Louis Aragon
– *pl.* the only oppressed group in our society that lives in intimate association with their oppressors
Evelyn Cunningham
– something that gets mad when you try to define it
Piet Grijs
– *pl.* the best other sex men have
Don Herold
– the second most important item in a bedroom
Paul Hogan
– the only exploited group in history who have been idealised into powerlessness
Erica Jong
– the nigger of the world
Yoko Ono
– the peg on which the wit hangs his jest, the preacher his text, the cynic his grouch and the sinner his justification
Helen Rowland
– a primitive animal who micturates once a day, defecates once a week, menstruates once a month, parturates once a year and copulates whenever she has the opportunity
W Somerset Maugham
– the eternal question, and man is the answer to it
Sidney Tremayne
(see also *beautiful woman, charming woman, faithful woman, good women, intelligent woman, liberated woman, successful woman, talkative woman, voluptuous woman*)

woman driver – one who drives like a man and gets blamed for it
Patricia Ledger

woman's intuition – often nothing more than man's transparency
George Jean Nathan

words – awkward instruments and they will be laid aside eventually, probably sooner than we think
William S Burroughs
– the great foes of reality
Joseph Conrad
– form the thread on which we string our experiences
Aldous Huxley
– the most powerful drug used by mankind
Rudyard Kipling
– often the gossips of our thoughts
Magdalena Samozwaniec

words

– loaded pistols
Jean-Paul Sartre
– vehicles that can transport us from the drab sands to the dazzling stars
M Robert Syme
– light things that change nothing
Jeanette Winterson

work – a dull way to get rich
Neal Ascherson
– a good way to keep busy
Herman Brusselmans
– the thing that interferes with golf
Frank Dane
– a form of nervousness
– the greatest thing in the world. So we should save some of it for tomorrow
Don Herold
– the only dirty four-letter word in the language
Abbie Hoffman
– the province of cattle
Dorothy Parker
– what is accomplished by those employees who have not yet reached their level of incompetence
Laurence J Peter
– the crab grass in the lawn of life
Charles Schulz
– a drug that dull people take to avoid the pangs of unmitigated boredom
W Somerset Maugham
– just another of man's diseases and prevention is better than cure
Heathcote Williams

workaholic – someone who says: 'Thank God It's Monday!'
Jerry Banks

working girl – one who quit her job to get married
E J Kiefer

work of art – part of nature seen through a temperament
André Gide

world – a stage with many lousy actors
Johan de Coninck
– a vast house of assignation to which the filing system has been lost
Quentin Crisp

– a cesspool of buffoonery
Chester Himes
– a prison in which solitary confinement is preferable
Karl Kraus
– proof that God is a committee
Bob Stokes
– a funny paper read backwards – and that way it isn't so funny
Tennessee Williams
– everything that is the case
Ludwig Wittgenstein
(see also *ideal world*)

worry – today's mouse eating tomorrow's cheese
Larry Eisenberg
– the interest paid by those who borrow trouble
George W Lyon

wrath – the anger of the upper classes
Jacqueline Gurnari

writer – *pl.* people that are always selling somebody out
Joan Didion
– a two-way channel, who must humbly offer the use of his voice to the life everlasting
William Gerhardi
– someone for whom writing is much harder than it is for the others
Ken Laws
– an ordinary guy who happens to write well
John O'Hara
– the engineer of the human soul
Joseph Stalin
– *pl.* people that are a little below the clowns and a little above the trained seals
John Steinbeck
– a reader turned inside out
John Updike
(see also *author, co-author, freelance writer, novelist, poet, professional writer*)

writing – a process of elimination
Martha Albrand
– a lonely and private substitute for conversation
Brooks Atkinson
– a metier that one learns by writing
Simone de Beauvoir
– nothing more than a guided dream
Jorge Luis Borges

– one thought after another dying on the one before
Mel Brooks
– one of the few professions in which you can psychoanalyze yourself, get rid of hostilities and frustrations in public, and get paid for it
Octavia Butler
– looking with closed eyes
Remco Campert
– turning one's worst moments into money
J P Donleavy
– mainly an attempt to out-argue one's past
Jules Feiffer
– swimming under water and holding your breath
F Scott Fitzgerald
– is to stare at a blank sheet of paper until drops of blood form on your forehead
Gene Fowler
– putting one's obsessions in order
Jean Grenier
– a voyage of discovery, like life itself
Henry Miller
– the hardest way of earning a living, with the possible exception of wrestling alligators
Olin Miller
– a dialogue between the writer and the society
Tess Onwueme
– one-tenth perspiration and nine-tenths masturbation
Joe Orton
– to give another body to your soul
Connie Palmen
– not a profession but a vocation of unhappiness
Georges Simenon
– a form of self-flagellation
William Styron
– practically the only activity a person can do that is not competitive
Paul Theroux
(see also *art of writing, major writing*)

WYMI – the all-philosophy radio station
Mike Dugan

x

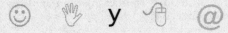

x – the folding chair of the alphabet
Ramón Gómez de la Serna

xerox – a trademark for a photocopying device that can make rapid reproductions of human error, perfectly
Merle L Meacham

x-ray – a device which enables us to see how the bones in the back room are doing
Don Quinn

xylophone – instrument developed at the request of Daniel Webster so there would be a word beginning with X in his dictionary
Cy DeBoer

y

yacht – boat with an attitude
Cy DeBoer

yawn – a silent shout
G K Chesterton

yes – the last word of the free life
Piet Grijs
– the best answer to an indecent proposal
Yvonne Kroonenberg

yodelling – hogcalling with frost on it
George M Cohan

yoghurt – the only poisoned drink that lengthens life
Fernand Auwera
– one of only three foods that taste exactly the same as they sound. The other two are goulash and squid
Henry Beard
– milk emeritus
Colin Bowles

youth – that part of society that hasn't got time yet to prove they are wrong
C Buddingh'
– the smile on Nature's face
Karel Boullart
– a period of missed opportunities
Cyril Connolly
– a disease from which we all recover
Dorothy Fuldheim
– the time when the stomach and chest occupy different parts of the body
Faith Hines
– a religion from which one always ends up being converted
André Malraux
– period that ends when you make relations instead of friends
Clem Schouwenaars
– a man or woman before it is fit to be seen
Evelyn Waugh

yuppie – a young and fluid creature, generally wanting in identity, that succeeds by studiously mimicking the members of its species that have already succeeded
Rick Bayan

Z

zeal – the necessary condition for becoming a zealot, which is remarkably close to being an idiot
Edmund H Volkart

zealot – a woman who irons her husband's socks
Cy DeBoer

zebra – a bar-coded horse
Mike Barfield
– a sports-model jackass
Milton Berle

Zen – a way of liberation, concerned not with discovering what is good or bad or advantageous, but what is
Alan Watts

Zeus – the god of wine and whoopee
Garrison Keillor

zigzag – the shortest distance between two bars
L L Levinson

zip code – a numerical system introduced by the US Postal Service to make sure that prompt delivery of mail will be further delayed
Edmund H Volkart

zipper – two rows of unsmiling teeth that often induce laughter in others esp. when inadvertently left open following a trip to the toilet
Rick Bayan

zoo – the place where your child asks loud questions about the private parts of large mammals
Joyce Armor
– an excellent place to study the habits of human beings
Evan Esar
– a place devised for animals to study the habitats of human beings
Oliver Herford
– an animal slum
Desmond Morris
– where the deer and the antelope stay
Roxanne Sayler Henke